MW00653571

Recalibrate
the
Culture

Recalibrate the Culture

Our Why...Our Work...
Our Values

Jimmy Casas

ConnectEDD Publishing
Hanover, Pennsylvania

Copyright © 2022 by Jimmy Casas

All rights reserved. No part of this publication may be reproduced, distributed, or transmitted in any form or by any means, including photocopying, recording, or other electronic or mechanical methods, without the prior written permission of the publisher, except in the case of brief quotations embodied in critical reviews and certain other noncommercial uses permitted by copyright law. For permission requests, contact the publisher at: info@connecteddpublishing.com

This publication is available at discount pricing when purchased in quantity for educational purposes, promotions, or fundraisers. For inquiries and details, contact the publisher at: info@connecteddpublishing.com

Published by ConnectEDD Publishing LLC
Hanover, PA
www.connecteddpublishing.com

Cover Design: Kheila Dunkerly

Recalibrate the Culture/ Jimmy Casas. —1st ed.
Paperback ISBN 979-8-9860690-5-0

Praise for *Recalibrate the Culture*

Jimmy Casas and his latest book, *Recalibrate the Culture*, provides practical examples of creating a school culture in which educators want to work and, more importantly, students can succeed. This book is a must-read for those working in education at every level!

—Chris Singleton | Author, and Inspirational Keynote Speaker

Recalibrate the Culture is the perfect book for this moment in education. Whether you are a superintendent, principal, teacher, or any other person who has dedicated themselves to making a positive difference in the lives of students, this book is for you. *Recalibrate the Culture* is filled with pertinent stories, practical examples, and actionable strategies for all educators.

—Anthony McConnell | Author, and Superintendent - Lemont-Bromberek Combined School District 113A

In *Recalibrate the Culture*, Jimmy Casas asks us to look within and consider our purpose, to look at each challenge and opportunity through the eyes of those with whom we share common goals, and to have the courage and humility needed to empower others. Casas's willingness to make himself vulnerable and to share his own struggles should serve as a guidepost for all educators.

—Dr. David C. Jeck | Superintendent, Fauquier County Public Schools

When I think of people who have impacted the trajectory of my career, Jimmy Casas is one of the first names that comes to mind. His ideas are some of the most innovative and heartfelt. His newest book, *Recalibrate the Culture*, might just be his best yet! Filled to the brim with resources that I find myself dying to try out. This book is one that should be added to every educator's library.

—Todd Nesloney | Director of Culture & Strategic Leadership at TEPSA

Jimmy Casas has captured the essence of solution-based leadership and the excellence that can exist in education. *Recalibrate the Culture* is prescriptive, timeless, and relevant to every school district that wants to go from a culture of surviving to thriving.

—Clint Pulver | Emmy Award-Winning Speaker and Best-Selling Author of "I Love It Here"

The title says it all and could not be more timely for educators: *Recalibrate the Culture*. The detrimental effects of the Covid-19 Pandemic have disillusioned many educators in our work. Through heartfelt and impactful stories combined with the Four Premises of *Culturize*, Jimmy Casas thoughtfully reminds us to reframe our thinking and recalibrate our work no matter our role in education. *Recalibrate the Culture* is the book all educators need in their hands for personal and school transformation. It's time to recalibrate ourselves and each other to live out a great story!

—Zac Bauermaster | Principal, Speaker, and Author of *Leading with a Humble Heart*

Recalibrate the Culture takes educators on a critical journey of self-reflection and vulnerability. Jimmy brings to light the challenges we face in our work today and provides valuable strategies to help all educators, regardless of their position, approach things differently. I can't tell you how many times I left a student, parent, teacher, or PD meeting, and thought, "That did not go well." This book took me back to those moments and created a vulnerable space to reflect and uncover what I could have and should have done differently. What I appreciate is that not only does Jimmy give you practical frameworks for reframing your personal leadership through scenarios we are all facing, but he also talks you through why the shift works. I needed this book at this critical time in education because it reminded me to invest in myself and live up to my principles so that I can make the impact I set out to make when I started my career as an educator.

—Shannon Myers | Assistant Superintendent, Bermudian
    Schools, PA

It's no secret to educators everywhere that this work is really hard, and the past few years seem to have exacerbated this. *Recalibrate* came just in time to remind me why I get up every day and give me the inspiration to recommit to this hard, but oh-so-important, work. Jimmy not only motivates, but he also provides numerous strategies, activities, and frameworks to help school leaders reconnect with their purpose and bring their teams along with them in this book. It's like having your very own school leadership coach by your side, that you can turn to in various situations time and time again.

—Katie Ritter, EdD | Chief Learning Officer, Forward Edge

Recalibrate the Culture offers a timely and much-needed commentary on the nuanced state that so many educators find themselves in and what to do about it. This book focuses on the fact that "who we are is how we lead" and the importance of making sure that we focus on ourselves as well as others. It is practical, inspiring, relevant, and needed! I encourage all educators to read this book and reframe their thinking on how they can best show up in their professional lives.

—LaNesha Tabb | Author, Educator, Speaker

In *Recalibrate the Culture*, Jimmy Casas challenges us as educators to not let trying times redefine who we are as leaders, but to reignite the flame of our why and use that passion and love to generate a school culture that excels. This book is a must read for all teachers and educational leaders. Whether you are in your first year or a veteran of education, *Recalibrate the Culture* will not only challenge and push you, but simultaneously reinvigorate your spirit and rekindle that fire that once drove you into this work.

—Jonathan Alsheimer | Teacher, Speaker, and Author

There is no doubt that the subject of recalibration has been front and center in conversations taking place in faculty meetings, administrative meetings, and board meetings all over our country. The question is, how will we reset?

Recalibrate the Culture is a needed resource to help educators refocus and reset. Jimmy Casas takes on this question and many more by providing leaders with practical tools and protocols to help educators heal from post pandemic systemic trauma.

This book is a must read for any leader or educator seeking an opportunity to rethink and refocus on the great work that they do every day to support students, teachers, and the larger educational community.

—Dr. Monica Batiste | retired Associate Superintendent of
Human Resources and Talent Management- Gwinnett County
Public Schools

Time to ditch those anonymous surveys. *Recalibrate the Culture* will refuel the "Why" behind your passion as an educator. This book is right on time reminding us that healthy, recalibrated educators are the key to a healthy culturized school. It is time to recalibrate yourself. Recalibrate your team. Recalibrate your culture.

—Marlon Styles | Superintendent, Middletown Community
Schools

Across the education world, we've been discussing things like "back to normal, reset, new normal" and the like. In *Recalibrate the Culture*, Jimmy Casas narrows the focus for educators everywhere as we move forward. Just as he brought *Culturize* and its four premises to the minds of educators in his first book, Jimmy asks educators and schools to examine what they value and recalibrate to meet the needs of our children. Jimmy's message, always authentic and real, resonates as a path forward from our recent past and on to a brighter future.

—Dr. Mark Wilson | National Principal of the Year (NASSP, 2009), Author, and Teacher of Leaders.

Recalibrate the Culture is a vivid reminder about the importance of relationships. Jimmy gives the reader tangible strategies that are inclusive of all stakeholders, focused on core values, and intentional on building connections that positively impact school culture using a tactical approach.

—Jerry Almendarez | Superintendent, Santa Ana U.S.D.

Jimmy does it again! He exquisitely captures the very essence of our collective purpose and passion for this work while providing a sustainable blueprint for recalibrating the culture that drives relational outcomes for all those we serve!

—Dr. Daniel M. Cullen | Special Education Administrator - Northeastern Pennsylvania

Recalibrate the Culture by Jimmy Casas is a timely resource for school leaders in this ever-changing environment within the educational atmosphere. The book focuses on four premises for leaders to earnestly contemplate in order to cultivate a culture at all levels of education—for the classroom, the school campus, and the district. Casas urges leaders to recalibrate internally and collectively to move and grow forward together, and together, rekindle the passion for serving the children within our schools.

—Dr. Alice Lee | Educator and Author

Throwing out best practices and the norms of the past is essential if we're going to be successful in a post-pandemic world and if we expect our students to successfully compete in a future-focused, global setting. Launching bold, actionable steps aimed at working together as systems on behalf of our school communities is paramount in our society. *Recalibrate the Culture* addresses just that, providing the reader with a treasure trove of "how to's" to help create a paradigm shift not only for a positive school culture, but also for the health and well-being of any administrator, building leader, or teacher leader.

—Daniel A. Domenech | Executive Director, AASA, The School
    Superintendents Association

Jimmy writes from a place of honesty and action. His ideas are always practical but also come with heart. This book really builds on the foundation of his first book *Culturize* and gives leaders everyday strategies to build an inclusive environment and purpose-driven support for their staff. A must-read for any district or campus leader!

—Carl Hooker, Educator/Entrepreneur

Dedication

This book is dedicated to every educator who sat in
the interview chair and visualized themselves changing the
trajectory of the life of a child. I hope you never doubt your impact.
Keep believing. This profession needs you.
Our kids need you. We need you.

Table of Contents

CHAPTER 1

Introduction

Who we are is how we lead...so we must always
focus on ourselves as well as others.

I t is time to recalibrate our culture. Recalibrate our why. Our work. Our values. Ourselves. Educators across the country are frustrated, exhausted, worried, angry, and bitter. I know that feeling all too well. I know from personal experience how demanding this work can be and what it can do to us—it can make us question, create doubt, change the core of who we are, and turn us into someone we no longer recognize. We are all vulnerable. The emotional toll of this job can cause us to lose our way. At one point in my own career, I lost my way and will forever be grateful to those who helped me find my way back.

Jim was one of those individuals who lifted me up. The district hired him to serve as my leadership coach. His job entailed monthly visits to my school to observe me in my capacity as a building principal and provide feedback. I was not thrilled about the idea of a stranger shadowing me throughout the school day. I was not in a good place at the time. My attitude was poor, my morale was at an all-time low, and I was depleted. Truthfully, I felt hopeless. I had grown tired of the political nature of the position and found myself growing more and more frustrated and impatient each day with different members of my school community and couldn't see things getting any better. I knew—based on his depth of knowledge, coupled with his experience and skill-set—that Jim was someone I could learn from, specifically, how to think and respond differently as a leader. But I was reluctant to admit that I was struggling.

One day I found myself frustrated with one of our staff members and complained to Jim, saying I couldn't understand how anyone would want to be a teacher and not love kids. He reminded me that we had hired this particular teacher and asked how it was possible that this same individual we thought so highly of in the interview room was now considered ineffective and someone who should no longer be employed as a teacher.

He then stated, "What if he isn't the problem? What if it is us? What if you looked at it differently?" Jim had a way of asking me questions that pushed me to reflect on my leadership.

"What do you mean?" I asked.

"Well Jimmy, let me ask you this," he said. "Why do you believe he is behaving in this manner? What do you know about him? Do you know his story? What processes are in place to help him continue to improve and grow as a teacher? Does he know what is expected of him? What supports were in place to support him once he was brought on board? It is easy to look at him today and blame him for his shortcomings, but I don't believe he wants to be ineffective. Based on what you are telling me, it is clear that he is struggling, but the question is why?"

The more questions Jim asked, the more I talked, the more he listened, and the more it became clear I was so frustrated with the teacher that it was easy to blame him rather than try to understand the reasons behind his behavior.

Jim helped me see it differently. I can't recall why Jim's words resonated with me so clearly at that moment, but I do remember the feeling I had after our conversation. I felt validated, encouraged, energized, and yet challenged–challenged in a way that made me want to be better. For the first time in a long time, I felt hopeful again. I felt recalibrated.

After years of doing my best to incorporate the many lessons that Jim and others taught me, many of which I still hold onto tightly today, I wrote *Culturize: Every Student. Every Day. Whatever It Takes.* (2017). Over 240,000 copies have been sold since its publication, resulting in thousands of teachers and campus leaders across the globe sharing their stories of how they transformed their campus cultures by anchoring their work in the four Premises of *Culturize*, specifically, leading from a core set of values.

In the spring of 2020, educators across the country would experience a brutal awakening in the form of a global pandemic that would shake our profession to its core. Suddenly, every decision that school leaders made was being questioned. Consequently, most struggled with what to do. The feeling among many educators is that most school districts were provided little support or guidance on how to move forward. Shaken but determined, our students, teachers, school/district leaders, and families did the best they could under the most dire circumstances imaginable. Ultimately, the pressure and stress from the countless hours that our educators were pouring in to navigate this treacherous course proved to be too much for many educators and schools as they continued to face the second wave of unknowns throughout the 2021-22 school year. Add to this the never-ending scrutiny, criticisms, and even threats spewed on our fellow educators across the country, and they had, well, a glut of other issues to contend with as a result of this crisis that, quite frankly, left many school communities somewhat traumatized.

During this period of trials and tribulations, I was in daily conversations with school leaders across the country who reached out to us seeking ways to help their students and staff fight through these unprecedented times. For those of you who may not know me, I have been an educator for over thirty years, starting as a middle school teacher in the inner-city schools of Milwaukee and eventually serving as a school administrator for twenty-two years. In 2012, I was named the Iowa Principal of the Year and in 2013, I was named the National Association of Secondary School Principals (NASSP) National Runner-Up Principal. In 2014, I was invited to the White House to speak on the Future Ready Pledge. In 2016, partly inspired by my experience with Jim, I started J Casas and Associates, a Leadership Coaching Company aimed at supporting school leaders and teachers across the country. Hence, the reason for schools contacting me seeking our advice and resources.

Although many schools may not have had a blueprint for how to navigate the plethora of challenges they were facing, we saw evidence everywhere of school communities responding quickly to keep students actively engaged in their learning. Within days, we witnessed schools and teachers shift to online learning opportunities for all students, staff members car-pooling through neighborhoods to remind their students how much they were missed, countless free meals provided to students and families who may have otherwise struggled to keep their children fed, and many teachers being provided flexible work options based on their health concerns just to name a few of the immediate steps that were taken to cope with the sudden pandemic. Despite these and countless other creative efforts to keep morale high and students and staff moving forward in a positive way, many schools sank to new lows on their overall climate and culture surveys. Yet, others remained more stable and in some cases, cultivated a culture that measured even higher than it had prior to the pandemic.

It is these types of mixed results that have driven my work the last few years with teachers, leaders, and schools across the country, assessing what it is that makes a difference in the overall culture of a school.

Why do some schools' learning data show positive outcomes across the board while others struggle to maintain a healthy learning environment for all students and staff. Pause for a moment and reflect on the following questions:

As a staff....

+ *Have some individuals reached a point in their careers where they are questioning if they can continue to do this work and whether it is even worth it anymore? More specifically, have you reached that point?*

+ *Have you taken inventory lately of what you value when it comes to the culture of your school?*

+ *Are you paying attention to whether your behavior reflects the core values that were created to help you define the standard of how adults are to treat students and colleagues in your organization?*

+ *Are you willing to allow individuals to continue to behave in ways that do not align with shared school values and then complain and, in some cases, label them when their behavior falls short of expectations?*

+ *Are you willing to invest time in people, listening to their experiences to help you understand why they behave the way they behave?*

+ *Does your district operate as a school system or a system of independent schools? Are your district office, school buildings, and classrooms aligned in their expectations and practices?*

The thought of our educators ever questioning whether they are making a difference or doubting whether it is worth all their hard work is both heartbreaking and gut-wrenching at the same time. If you are still here with me, my hope is it is because you still believe in what you are doing and just need a recalibration of sorts. I believe in you, and I believe in our work as teachers and school leaders, and I know without a doubt we are making a difference every day. Take a moment and think about how many times in your career you have received an email from a former student thanking you for making a difference in their lives. What about the students that return to your classroom or school years later to visit you and thank you? Or the former students and colleagues who reach out in their time of need for advice, or a letter of recommendation? What about the countless others who follow you or connect with you on social media? And wedding invitations? OMG! Those are the best!

To no longer believe in what we are doing would be a hopeless existence and we are not hopeless, my friends. We chose this profession because we believed we could make a difference and I am asking you to believe you are and still can. I offer you all the grace in the world because I believe you are doing the best you can with what you know and the resources you have.

So, let's take inventory of where you currently are. If you are one of those educators who is currently feeling overwhelmed, exhausted, depleted, or wondering whether you can continue to do this work, I am going to ask you to visualize yourself back in the interview chair and remind you that someone hired you because they believed in you. They heard your words, they saw your passion, and they felt your heart. You were genuine and sincere, and you convinced a group of people that you were the best person for the job, and you sincerely believed it. That is the real you. Go back and find yourself in that interview again to re-establish, rekindle, reignite, and remind yourself why you wanted to become an educator.

The Four Premises of *Culturizing* a Positive School Culture

A healthy culture is critical to the success of any organization. A healthy work culture is one in which you look forward to going to each day because you feel connected, valued, appreciated, and inspired. You are given a voice to be a part of something bigger, something meaningful, and you believe that together with your colleagues, you can accomplish anything.

I hope to take the 4 Premises of *Culturize* to help you **recalibrate** your workplace culture into a healthy, thriving culture. I hope to do so in a way that allows you to bring the best version of yourself to the members of your school community so they, in turn, can do the same for others. I am also going to challenge you to see things differently than you currently see them–to **reframe** them for yourself and others.

Recalibrate: to start over again from a fresh point of reference to bring a newfound sense of hope and positively impact morale.

Reframe :to see things differently; to see how our behavior impacts others and that, by changing our behavior, we can generate better results.

You will see these two terms used throughout the book and I hope that you will embed them into your work and utilize them as a springboard to positive change for yourself, your staff, and your culture. Shouldn't every student, every teacher, every support staff person, and every school and district leader have access to and be given the necessary support to ensure their success? I believe so and I think you do, too.

The primary purpose of this book is to assist all teachers, principals, and district office administrators in exploring their inner selves to understand the role we each play in terms of impacting the climate and culture of an entire campus when we are strategic and aligned in our practices. The classroom, building, and district levels must see themselves as one and must be intentional in replicating the processes, protocols, and frameworks provided in this book to recalibrate and bring about system-wide change and cultivate a healthier culture.

In the subsequent chapters of this book, I will expand on the four premises of *culturizing* a positive school culture to assist you in bringing about systemic change. It is also written in a way to get you to reflect on your behaviors and responses so you can begin to identify where you can move forward to becoming a better version of yourself, both in your professional and personal life. To get started, here is a summary of the Four Premises from *Culturize*:

To start, we must **Lead from a Core Set of Values**. This begins with knowing who we are as individuals and what we believe in as an organization. Core values are the fiber of everything we believe in and everything we do. Effective educators lead in a way where their behaviors mirror the established values they have formed for themselves. These values are then carried into the school environment and aligned with their work. With their peers, they begin to identify and define their values as a collective group and then do their very best to align their actions to these agreed-upon principles. These committed individuals do not allow their colleagues to stray from these values and act in ways that inspire others to do the same.

Next, we must **Cultivate a Community of Leaders**. I think we must always begin with the belief that everyone can lead. Period. Effective leaders focus on growing leaders, and they are intentional in developing the capacity of others in their organization to encourage, support, invite and inspire others to lead with them. They view themselves as teachers and coaches and invest their time in others by listening to their stories to better understand their passions, talents, dreams, concerns, and fears. The better they know the people they are serving, the more they can elevate them so others can experience their own success.

In addition to leading from a core set of values and cultivating a community of leaders, all staff members **See the Culture Through the**

Eyes of Others. These forward-thinking educators recognize they will not always see the potential issues coming their way. They are strategic in their approach to avoiding potential culture killers. They build trust by permitting others to help them see blind spots that they don't see, especially when the pace and stress of the job becomes overwhelming.

Finally, healthy cultures understand that **Average Exists in Every Organization.** No school campus is immune to this. However, high-performing cultures do not allow average to become the standard. They are intentional in putting processes, protocols, frameworks, and systems into place to identify, define, and—most importantly—do something about it because they know that low morale is the thief of a positive culture. They believe that everyone in the organization is responsible for morale and culture, and they implement effective processes for everyone to have a voice in putting a plan in place to address their average.

> Low morale is the thief of a positive culture.

4 PREMISES OF CULTURIZE

Live a Core Set of Values.	Cultivate a Community of Leaders
See Culture Through the Eyes of Others.	Average Exists in Every Organization.

For too long, we have been handed a set of keys to classrooms and schools and then left alone to figure out how to create an environment in which staff and students alike feel valued and appreciated and inspired to teach and learn. Can you imagine a doctor being handed a set of keys and then left alone to consult a patient? Sounds absurd, doesn't it? Yet, that is basically what we do to our teachers and principals. What if we re-examined our current systems to identify the inequities that currently exist in our classrooms and our schools? What would we find? I can tell you from my own experience what I encountered in my twenty-two years as a school leader and the work that I continue to do today as a Leadership Coach: that many of our classrooms and schools as they currently exist lack the necessary processes, protocols, and structures to be successful. What if we were able to provide our teachers and school/district leaders with a framework to help guide them in their inner work, and revitalize the entire campus?

I hope to illustrate how you can recalibrate a positive culture across all levels of the campus, from the classroom, to the building level, to the district office, by utilizing the Four Premises of *Culturize* as a framework to guide your work. The amount of time, energy, and emotion that you pour into this work can cause you to become someone you never intended to become, especially when you don't believe your efforts are producing the results you hoped to attain. This feeling of doubt can begin to creep inside your head and cause you to question your purpose, just like it did for me early on in my career when I did the best I could, but it never quite seemed to be enough.

I believe that by equipping our teachers and leaders with a new way of thinking and, more importantly, with strategies for approaching their work more intentionally and effectively, we can revitalize our schools and make an immediate positive impact on the culture of every classroom and school across the country.

I do not profess to have all the answers. I would never want to portray myself in that way. But I believe I can help you—not help you find the answers, but help you get better results by recalibrating your system and reframing your thinking. By recalibrating and reframing, you will strengthen your resolve and begin to see things differently and respond differently, and by doing so, you will become a better version of yourself.

As Jim reminded a young, frustrated leader many years ago, we must reframe our thinking so that we can continue to grow and develop in our responses and roles as educators. Our kids, colleagues, supervisors, and families deserve the best version of you. And guess what? So do you! If you are still reading this book, maybe, just maybe, it is because you know in your heart you are ready to recalibrate. So will you join me? If so, you can't "ish" it. You have to be all in. Effective educators are intentional, strategic, resilient, persistent, and self-aware. Your best thinking about teaching and leading has gotten you to this point. Now what?. Will you keep using only your own thinking or is it time to be more strategic and begin to encompass parts of someone else's thinking? My best thinking got me to this point as well. My hope is our thinking together about how we behave and lead will take us to the next level.

> Healthy cultures are transparent cultures and changing any culture starts with small steps across all levels.

Healthy cultures are transparent cultures and changing any culture starts with small steps across all levels. Let's work together to recalibrate our culture by reframing our thinking and *culturizing* our classrooms, our buildings, and our district offices.

Reflect AND
RECALIBRATE

(Use the following space for reflective notes)

CHAPTER 2

Premise 1: Lead From a Core Set of Values

When we come together as one,
we become the best of who we are.

The Core Values of *Culturize*

If you have seen the video of Clint Pulver and Mr. Jensen, (Pulver, 2017) you will probably recollect the moment when Mr. Jensen reaches into his desk and pulls out a set of drum sticks and looks at Clint, and says, " I don't think you are a problem; I think you are a drummer," and then proceeds to hand Clint his first pair of drumsticks. Every time I watch that video, the first thing I ask myself is, " I wonder how many drummers I placed in the hallway as a middle school teacher and scolded them? How many drummers did I send to the office because I was frustrated with their behavior? How many drummers did I fail because they weren't doing their homework? Regrettably, too many. I shared earlier in the introduction that I lost my way early on in my career because I forgot why I wanted to be a teacher. Ironically,

I went into education because I wanted to work with the "drummers" and yet, here I found myself resenting them. This would lead me down a path of behaving contrary to what I shared in my interview. Rather than being a champion for students and staff, I was quitting on them. I was asking students and teachers to do things that I wasn't doing myself and when I didn't get the results I expected, I pointed the finger at others and blamed them. Instead of taking responsibility for my failures, I convinced myself that I couldn't teach or lead people who didn't care or in some cases, didn't even want to try.

I still recall one of my mentors asking me, "What happened to the young man who came to the inner city to champion for kids who needed a champion? What happened to him? Where did he go? This doesn't sound like the same person I first met years ago." He was right, I was not in a good place and needed some guidance on where to go next. With his support, he helped me see myself back in the interview chair so I could recalibrate my why and become the leader I always wanted to be. Although I knew it was not going to be easy, after seeking his advice it was clear what I was going to have to do—I was going to have to change me. Over the next few months, I began to develop what today are the Core Principles of *Culturize*, which, I believe, gave me the foundation to become a more effective leader and—more importantly—created a framework to hold myself accountable for my purpose, my behavior, and my results. To this day, I aim to use these principles in every aspect of my life, both professionally and personally. By no means do these principles exonerate me from having some not-so-great moments, but they do serve as a constant reminder of the leader and person I want to be.

> Regardless of our role, we can all benefit by periodically recalibrating our purpose.

Although the example above comes from my lens as a building principal, titles are irrelevant when it comes to visualizing oneself in the interview chair. Regardless of our role, we can all benefit by periodically recalibrating our purpose.

CULTURIZE CORE PRINCIPLES

CHAMPION FOR STUDENTS

Never quit on a student. When a student doesn't meet your expectations, **invest more time to understand their story**. Show compassion and empathy. When we take time to connect to their experiences, it shows we value them and their voice.

EXPECT EXCELLENCE

What we model is what we get. **Model the behaviors you want others to emulate.** We should never ask others to do what we are not willing to do ourselves. Every school has average, but the best schools do not allow average to become the standard.

CARRY THE BANNER

Be a positive voice at all times for your students, colleagues, and families. Do your best to **create meaningful experiences** with those whom you come in contact with so when they walk away, they speak positively about their interaction with you.

MERCHANT OF HOPE

Believe that everyone wants to be great. No student, parent, or staff member wants to be a failure. However, there will be times when people lose their way. **Believe that you can inspire others** to be more and do more than they ever thought possible.

Every Student. Every Day. Whatever It Takes.

As you progress through this book, you will see these four principles woven throughout each chapter in no particular order. Like any good teacher, I want to invest time in you because I know you want to be great. It is important to me that you see and understand my rationale for why it is important to have a framework to help guide you so you don't lose your way. I don't want to tell you what you should do; rather, I want to create an experience for you in such a way that if you like what you see and read, you will think positively about it and you will want to replicate it.

Did you see it? The principles of *Culturize* are woven in the paragraph above. That is what I hope to accomplish throughout the book so they become encompassed in every aspect of your work, regardless of

> Culture is not about one thing. It is about everything.

your role or title. To maximize your impact on the culture you have to see beyond doing one thing differently. Culture is not about one thing. It is about everything.

Let me list the four core principles of *Culturize* and explain them for you more clearly:

Champion for Students: We will never quit on a student. When a student doesn't meet your expectations, invest more time to understand their story. Show compassion and empathy. When we take time to connect to their experiences, it shows we value them and their voice.

Expect Excellence: We will model the behaviors we want others to emulate. What we model is what we get. We should never ask others to do what we are not willing to do ourselves. Average exists in every school, but the best schools do not allow average to become the standard.

Carry the Banner: We will be a positive voice at all times for our students, colleagues, and families. Do your best to create meaningful experiences with people you come in contact with so that when they walk away, they speak positively about their interactions with you.

Merchant of Hope: We believe that everyone wants to be great at what they do. No student, parent, or staff member wants to be a failure. However, there will be times when people lose their way. Believe that you can inspire others to be more and do more than they ever thought possible.

I am not proposing that you or your school adopt the Core Principles of *Culturize*, although schools have done so. I am suggesting that you work with your staff to create a framework that identifies and defines the values of your organization to help guide you in living out those principles daily, holding yourselves accountable for behaviors and commitments that will lead you to the level of excellence that you aspire to achieve. Before you take the next step, we will need to stop and reflect on how we are currently treating the people in our organization.

You Can't Outsource Relationships to Others

Relationships. Relationships. Relationships. It has been stated countless times that the foundation of every healthy culture begins and ends with relationships. As educators, we are in the people business. When a child feels connected, capable, and confident, anything is possible. The same is true for adults. In the best classrooms, every student feels like a favorite student. In the best schools, every staff member feels like a favorite as well. Hence, why we must always take care of our people. Imagine a school where every student has a friend to sit with at lunch, play with at recess, or connect with in PE, and a classmate or teacher they can trust when they need someone to talk to or help with their schoolwork. Imagine a place where staff members have colleagues to join them for lunch, to talk about their lesson planning, and who check on them or invite them to happy hour. Is every student and staff member in your school having this experience? If not, what potential perils loom for all of us? What can we do to resolve the situation?

The last few years have been a rude awakening for educators everywhere. The danger of teacher and leader burnout, especially for those who were once on fire, is real, my friends. The demands that are being placed on all educators are daunting. Teachers are certainly feeling it, as evidenced by the increase in teachers leaving the profession, but if we look closely, our principals and superintendents are feeling it as well. And let's not forget our students and families. Everyone is feeling the stress.

Chronic Stress Effects

Did you know...?

- Chronic stress affects motivation. (Morgado P and Cerqueira JJ (2018) Editorial: The Impact of Stress on Cognition and Motivation. Front. Behav. Neurosci. 12:326. doi: 10.3389/fnbeh.2018.00326)

- Being in close contact with stressed people increases your stress levels. (Bains, 2018)

- Stress impairs self-control. (Maier, et al, 2015)

- Stress impairs memory. (Yuen et al, 2012)

- The hippocampus (the part of the brain that processes memory) is smaller in those with chronic stress. (Kim, et al, 2015)

- Dwelling on stressful events increases inflammation in the body. (Zoccola, et al, 2013)

- The amygdala part of the brain that modulates the fear response, is highly activated during times of stress. (Ressler KJ. Amygdala activity, fear, and anxiety: modulation by stress. Biol Psychiatry. 2010;67(12):1117–1119. doi:10.1016/j.biopsych.2010.04.027)

This past year I was working in a school district and the superintendent was airing her frustration about certain staff members. She shared with me that it didn't seem to matter how much she did for them, they still complained about a plethora of issues, including feeling overwhelmed and stressed regarding the number of extra things they were being required to do, which impacted morale among the staff. She became visibly and increasingly frustrated as she proceeded to rattle off several things they had done to combat these issues, including extra jeans days, wellness events, mental health days, additional preps, and a reduction in duties. We know that these and other similar practices can have an immediate short-term positive effect on staff morale, but it has proven time and again that the benefit does not endure when we fail to change the way we treat others in our organizations. Added life stresses don't just come from more work being piled on people; they are also compounded when people are treated in ways that devalue them. Effective teachers and leaders understand that it is not only what we know about our students and colleagues, but how we treat them that determines how healthy our classroom, building, and district office culture is. In this case, the district still had a ways to go in how staff felt they were being treated by the administration and vice versa. Reframing our thinking will help us see that how we treat people in our schools can have a detrimental impact on staff morale and lead to an unhealthy culture.

> Added life stresses don't just come from more work being piled on people; they are also compounded when people are treated in ways that devalue them.

Below is an excerpt from a current award-winning educator who shared the following story with me regarding her experience as a classroom teacher. It serves as a reminder that even successful teachers at times bear the burden of intense scrutiny that can make them question whether they can continue in their role:

My name is Monica and I am a 7th-grade teacher in a mid-sized, suburban district. I have been blessed in my educational career to teach the most precious children, work with inspiring colleagues, and receive several awards. Two years ago, I was named my county's Teacher of the Year and last year, finished runner-up for state Teacher of the Year. This recognition was the most prestigious honor of my professional career. It was also the year I considered leaving the profession.

I'm grateful that I had several joyful years of teaching under my belt before the profession was turned upside down. The pandemic drastically changed the profession in ways that I could have

---

never imagined. Contract hours went from blurred to obsolete. Phone calls, texts, emails, and all other forms of communication between colleagues, administrators, parents, and even students were expected at all hours of the day and night to "do what was best for children." Constant changes in expectations, teaching modalities, and responsibilities made every "pivot" feel like another crack in my once beloved and joyful career. To top it all off, every single moment felt like a make-or-break moment to teach and close the learning gap for my students.

The pressure to be a great teacher, to do what I know in my heart and professional opinion is best for children, and maintain a family, social, and personal life outside of school quickly became unmanageable. I went from a happy-go-lucky person who loved teaching with all of her heart to an anxious, moment-by-moment person who could barely get herself out of bed in the morning to make it to school. I was once a proud teacher who enjoyed the responsibilities and leadership roles I earned, but I quickly became bitter that I was drowning trying to balance everything, while a teacher down the hallway who was doing the bare minimum with zero leadership roles and responsibilities was receiving the same "proficient ratings" as I was on evaluations. I began to doubt my calling, my belief in my professional purpose, and my reason for teaching.

It took a major life event, changing my perspective, nearly six months of serious self-reflection, lots of prayers, and the support from my incredible family and husband to remind me of why I became a teacher. I became a teacher because I love teaching children. Not because I love the curriculum, leadership, or creating. I simply love children and I love teaching them. That's it. So to keep myself in this profession, I had to take a few giant steps back, put my purpose for teaching back at the forefront of my career, and, most importantly, put myself and my family first. Those last two things are irreplaceable. I respectfully stepped down from all leadership roles and responsibilities. I started saying no to things that did not bring me joy or positively impact the students in my classroom. I carefully protected my time outside of school.

After making these changes, I have found the "pre-pandemic joy" I referenced earlier. While last year I considered leaving the profession, this year I'm finally back to doing and believing in what I was called to do, while also living a fulfilling life outside of school.

Monica's experience reminds us how important it is for leaders to pour time into their relationships with staff to gauge their mental health and level of stress. The demands placed on educators ebb and flow throughout the year. This work cycle can negatively impact the morale of an entire campus, leaving people like Monica feeling drained, burned out, and at times, guilty. By taking time to recalibrate, she was able to place herself and her immediate family back into her inner circle and rekindle her love for teaching again.

The Power of Why x 3

In his book, *Start with Why: How Great Leaders Inspire Everyone to Take Action* (2011) Simon Sinek explains that "people don't buy what you do; they buy why you do it." He goes on to explain the secret ingredient behind successful leaders is the motivation behind their actions. Instead of thinking about what they do or how they do it, their focus is on the "why." In other words, the **Why of the Work.** What is your *purpose?* What is your cause, your belief? Why do you get out of bed in the morning? This does not apply solely to leaders, but teachers and yes, students, as well. I encounter students and educators on a daily basis who have lost their passion for their work and school in general. Students, teachers, and administrators who are walking into school each day, doing their best to get through the day, oftentimes checking the boxes, and then grinding their way until the end of the day. Sadly, they get up and do it all again the next day, like a music playlist on repeat.

I agree wholeheartedly with Sinek's thoughts on the power of this one simple, but powerful, word. However, over the last few years, I've reflected on Sinek's notion of "why" to see it as a framework to help reframe my thinking when it comes to the behavior of people in our organizations. My takeaway is that when it comes to leadership, if there is one thing that remains true after all these years, it is that people will behave however we allow them to behave.

> People will behave however we allow them to behave.

My intent is not to state that we should be controlling others; rather, it is to emphasize the importance of understanding the "why" behind someone's *behavior*–The **Why of the Response**. I believe that, at its core, culture equals behavior–look around and observe the behavior of students and staff members and that will tell us most of what we need to know about the culture of a school. However, in my experience, healthy cultures go beyond observation, investing time in others to understand the origin of their behavior. In other words, they are purposeful in building relationships with others to understand why people behave the way they behave. In *Culturize*, the 4th Core Principle reminds us that people want to be great at what they do. If students and staff are not performing at the level we want them to or expect them to, then we must try our best to understand the "Why?" behind their behavior. When we try to better understand the reason behind the behaviors of others, we are more equipped to provide guidance, influence thinking and emotions, and help reframe situations in a way that helps them discover a more positive path forward.

The third and final component of the *Power of Why* lies in the *task*– **The "Why" of the Change.** Too often we ask people to do something without clarity. When people don't understand the why behind a task or an initiative, they often will do it, but they will not be invested and, therefore, we will not achieve the result we hoped for. A lack of clarity when working with students, staff, and families promotes confusion, creates anxiety, and eventually causes them to hesitate for fear of doing something wrong.

> When we are intentional, we can help others find their way back to their why.

When you reflect on your students and staff who struggle, ask yourself, "Did I invest time to understand why they behave the way they do? Why do they no longer have a passion for learning or teaching? Why is their current behavior not at the level we expect it to be? Why are they not doing what we asked them to do?" We cannot allow our understanding of the *Power of Why* to be causal. When we are intentional, we can help others find their way back to their why.

Next time, start with this framework, but this time with the goal of helping understand why others behave the way they behave so you can inspire them back to greatness.

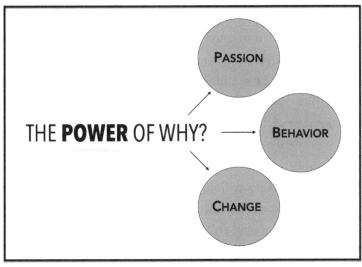

The Core Begins with You

If you are currently feeling stressed, overwhelmed, exhausted, frustrated, or any combination of these feelings, let's begin by reminding ourselves that we cannot fix or solve every dilemma that we encounter. That is not our responsibility. Our job is to change ourselves to see if we can get better and minimize these feelings so we can take a healthier version of ourselves to work and bring a better version of ourselves home each night.

Examine the visual graphic below. We begin with YOU. It is the center of the foundation because you are the most important part of this visual and you must, therefore, treat yourself accordingly. This begins by knowing yourself. Who are you? What do you value most? What is important to you? How are you behaving? Where and to whom are you giving your time, your most precious gift? I am asking you to recalibrate yourself by re-examining who and what is at the center of your core.

As you extend outward, reflect on who you have placed there. For many educators, the root of our stresses, pressures, and–may I add–feelings of guilt, begin here because of where we place our priorities. If you recall, this is where Monica found herself. Like Monica, many of us have convinced ourselves due to the demands of the job, that our students, staff, and community belong in our immediate circle. I am asking you to reconsider another viewpoint as illustrated below. The center of the first ring reminds us of our purpose, our why. Next to our purpose lies our spouse/significant other and our children. Should we not take care of our children and spouses by investing time and taking care of them before someone else's children, our friends, or even extended family? I think most would agree yet look at the actions of most educators and they will not mirror this belief. There will be times when we need to put our students in the inner ring, but if we keep them there longer than our own children, we risk losing precious moments with them that we can never recover. We often label ourselves as "bad educators" when we put our children first and I am here to tell you that you are not a bad educator. You are a responsible and loving parent who knows their core.

We have missed our exit along Priority Street and we have taken a different route; a route layered with gravel and orange construction signs warning us to slow down because of the dangers ahead, but we continue to ignore them until it is too late. Reframing our inner circle permits us to place students, staff, friends, extended family, and the community on the outer rings, free of guilt, and allows us to produce a healthier version of ourselves to begin to re-establish our collective commitments as a school community.

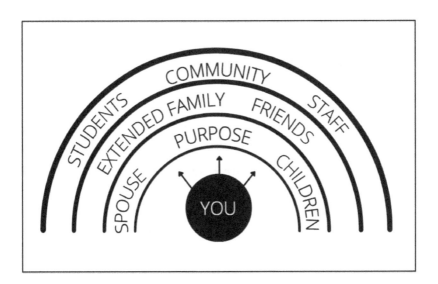

Revisiting Our Core Values

Earlier this year, I was working in an elementary school and as I walked down a hallway I noticed a large sign hanging on the wall that said, "Kindness Matters," and in smaller letters underneath read the phrase

"Treat others how you would want to be treated." It is not uncommon to see similar signs and words posted around a school building reminding all who enter what one can expect to see and experience upon entering and visiting the school.

Suddenly from around the corner, I heard an adult in an elevated voice yell, "Max, I've now told you three times to keep your hands to yourself and I am not going to tell you again. I'm tired of you, and your classmates are tired of you touching them. One more time and you are going to the office!" In ten seconds, the words that I had just read a moment earlier lost all meaning.

This interaction and others like it continue to play out each day in schools across the country. Maybe you have experienced a similar encounter that caused you to reflect on whether you should confront or ignore such behavior of a colleague. Regardless of which choice you made and how that choice made you feel, I wonder, "Do you wish that you could make that feeling go away?" Let's revisit the 2nd bulleted item back in the opening chapter:

+ *Are you paying attention to whether your behavior as a staff reflects the core values that were created to help you define the standard of how adults are to treat students and colleagues in your organization?*

It is important to note that during a school year we will find some students and staff members in a positive space, some feeling anxious, others physically and/or emotionally tired, and some in a state of all three combined, which ultimately can affect their behavior. As I just mentioned in the previous section, even more critical is knowing where people are on the continuum, how they landed there, and why. This is a reminder about the importance of investing time to get to know our students and staff–the *Power of Why*. Positively impacting all students and staff are best attained through collective commitments. No single person can reach all students or staff, but collectively we increase our chances exponentially.

> No single person can reach all students or staff, but collectively we increase our chances exponentially.

Like many of you, I have read hundreds of variations defining these collective commitments, usually in the form of mission, vision, and values statements. Most look and sound pretty much the same. Let's revisit the intent behind each of these:

Mission: Why - Why do we do what we do? What is our purpose as a school, as a staff?

Vision: What - What do we hope to become as a school?

Values: How - How will we behave collectively on a daily basis to achieve the vision and fulfill the mission?

If we look closely at the words above, then we should be excited about any school we enter that has taken the time to answer these three questions and whose behaviors align with their words. Unfortunately, we know this is not always the case. At some point we all need to ask ourselves this fundamental question: Have we taken the time to discuss these items and collectively agree as a staff on our purpose (why we exist), our vision (what we hope to become for our students, staff, and community), and how we will behave to achieve this. If so, then where does the disconnect begin? Why are we not getting the results we want in terms of our culture?

Let's begin by examining our behavior. We know that behavior is often predictable. Therefore, can we predict that all of us—yes all of us, me included—at some point, despite our best intentions, are going to violate the very agreements that we discussed, debated, word smithed, and agreed to. Why? Because we are not perfect beings. We get tired, we get frustrated, we label, and there are times we want to throw our hands up in the air and yell, "I quit!" You care so darn much about making sure that every student and every staff member reaches their full potential that when you start to see that you are not making progress to get them to that level, you begin to doubt that you can. One of the hardest things about being an educator is thinking that we are not able to reach a child and when we come to that moment, we are in danger of behaving in ways not aligned with our values. So if you agree that we can predict this, then let's change and reframe a new approach so we can achieve the results we hoped to achieve when we worked tirelessly as a staff to create a great culture.

Recalibrating Our Collective Commitments

Let's revisit the definition of healthy work culture: a place where you look forward to going each day because you feel connected, valued, appreciated, and inspired. You are given a voice to be a part of something bigger, something meaningful, and you believe that together with your colleagues, you can accomplish anything.

If you want to get people to invest in recalibrating their collective commitments, then you are going to need a process to ensure everyone has a collective voice. Teachers and support staff are more likely to put forth their best effort when they have a legitimate voice in the process. The same holds true for students and parents. Input matters. In the next section, I will dive deeper into a framework to help bring more clarity to this process and how we can go about ensuring everyone's voice is

> Teachers and support staff are more likely to put forth their best effort when they have a legitimate voice in the process.

heard. For now, let's go back and revisit the work we started above, focusing solely on the third commitment: *Values: How - How will we behave collectively on a daily basis to achieve the vision and fulfill the mission?*

Imagine for a moment a process in which the entire staff is placed into groups of four and given ample time to reflect, discuss, share out, and collaborate to come up with specific behaviors (values) that they believe would positively impact their classroom culture. After much discussion, the staff identifies three areas they are willing to commit to that they believe will bring about immediate change. Ironically, these three—relationships, engagement, and formative assessments—just so happen to be the same three areas that I believe will provide you better results when it comes to fostering a healthy classroom culture when implemented effectively.

By effectively, I mean first, we must define what we mean by these terms. Let's take relationships, for example. If we were to ask all four members in the groups above, my guess is we might get four different definitions of what we mean by relationships. How I define relationships may or may not align with the way others define the word. This immediately creates a disconnect in terms of how we will behave, how we go about building relationships with our students. As simple as this sounds, this step is often overlooked, creating a plethora of issues and frustrations among staff members right from the outset.

Next, we often leave out the crucial step of identifying specific and agreed-upon practical ways in which we will collectively and intentionally build relationships daily with our students. If this is never discussed and agreed upon upfront, then it is likely that some teachers will make this their focus and others will not. Others will do the best they know how, but if it fails to produce the expected results, they are likely to stop doing it. In my work, I have witnessed educators, teachers, principals, and district office staff spend an enormous amount of time, energy, and resources on training, yet they continue to fall short when it comes to getting the results they hoped to get.

Giving everyone a voice is critical in creating a healthy culture, but it does not necessarily guarantee a positive result. When everyone is given a voice as part of a process that clearly defines what our values mean and they are given a voice again to identify practical ways in which we all agree to live out those values (behaviors), then we benefit from better outcomes. However, to create a ripple effect across the entire system at all levels, the classroom teacher and district office personnel would have to reflect on the same steps above when working with students and principals, respectively.

Revisiting core values is the most critical component of any healthy culture, in my opinion; hence, why I opened the chapter with this premise first. We must reframe this process to lay the foundation so we can achieve a healthy and vibrant culture. As we noted earlier, **to reframe** means to see things differently; to see how our behavior impacts others and realizing that, by changing our behavior, we can generate better results. Let's continue with the third commitment to see how a change in our behavior can get us those better results.

If we can predict that at some point we will violate this, then let's take our *How* and expand on it even further. What I have learned in working through this process with staff is that we end the conversation too soon. Let's be honest. This can be grueling work and there comes a time when we are just ready to be done with this work and pat ourselves on the back because, on paper, it does look pretty darn good. However, by taking the *How* two steps further, it should—and in most cases does—culminate in a better result. Remember, we cannot fix and solve every person's behavior, student or staff, but we can change *our practices* and see positive changes. Those next two steps look like this:

How will we respond when the behavior of one of our students or colleagues doesn't align with the values that we collectively agreed to?

When educators invest time to collectively discuss this question and come to some agreements on what this will look like, it gives everyone in the organization permission to not confront or attack, but gently remind each other what everyone agreed to.

How will we respond when someone reminds us that our behavior isn't mirroring the collective agreements?

Will we get our feelings hurt? Will we get defensive? Will we get up and walk out because we didn't like that someone called us out? Or will we say thank you? Thank the individual for helping us, and for reminding us to be who we said we were going to be. This is where we hold ourselves accountable for our behavior and, more importantly, permit others to hold us accountable. Experience has taught me we all need it. Each of us has experienced moments when we have gotten defensive or had our feelings hurt because someone called us out. When this conversation is initiated up front and agreed to ahead of time, it reduces the tension and allows us to better accept the feedback because it has already been discussed and agreed to prior. It softens the message a bit and doesn't catch us off guard. They are called collective agreements or values for a reason—so we can collectively hold each other accountable to behave in a way that just doesn't talk about how "kindness matters" or to "treat others how you would want to be treated," but ensures that those words on a sign that hangs in your school truly mean something and represent who we are as educators. So if we want to make that feeling go away—the feeling that we are unsure what to say when someone's behavior is not aligned with our values or avoid it altogether—let's take time as a staff to recalibrate and revisit who we want to become.

These last two questions are critical in fostering a culture in which everyone is responsible for the culture of the school. Having conversations, taking our agreements further, and giving permission to others to help us be great will produce a healthier culture for all members of our school community.

1 - 2 - 4 Framework

In the previous section, staff members were placed in groups of four and given the task to define the word "relationships" and identify practical ways to build relationships collectively and intentionally with students.

Giving everyone a voice is a vital component of recalibrating a culture. When everyone is given a voice as part of a process, they are often more invested in the process and therefore, want to contribute to their quest to procure a more dynamic culture. In many instances, whether it be a classroom lesson, a building or district meeting, or committee meeting, only the voice of a few are taken into consideration. Students and parents share similar experiences regarding their student council and PTA/PTO meetings. Interestingly, teachers, principals, and superintendents open up the room for discussion, seek input, and allow for conversation, yet we continue to struggle when it comes to yielding positive results.

Why does this happen? It is because we perceive that everyone was given a *voice* when in fact they were only given a chance to *express their voice*. How often has the following scenario played out: The classroom teacher poses a question to the class and initially the response is crickets. The teacher repeats the question, hoping that this time she gets a response. Suddenly, a hand goes up and a student offers a comment. The teacher continues, hoping to get more volunteers. Another hand and then another hand. The teacher moves on after four to five answers, feeling good about what the students shared. Such responses are common in classrooms, conference rooms, and offices across campus. Although we convince ourselves that we have gathered ample feedback, the truth is we have not. What is lacking is an effective framework to ensure that everyone is actively engaged and authentically sharing their voice. The 1 - 2 - 4 framework is a productive way to improve collective input and almost always produces a better result when carried out effectively. An explanation is provided below:

To begin, place people in groups of four whenever possible. Groups of three will work but limit the size of the groups to no more than five. The larger the group, the more likely people will sit back or not be given equal opportunity to engage. Next, provide group members with paper, note cards, post-it notes, or electronic means to record responses. For this example, there are five groups of four teachers per table in a room (twenty teachers in total) and we plan to have them revisit the original challenge of defining relationships.

Framework: 1 - 2 - 4:

1 - Group members are given independent time to reflect and process the question, "How do you define relationships?" to generate the best response. In each group, all four members individually write out a response. This is important because it automatically gives every participant a voice in the process and it allows them time to pause, process, and reflect on the question and how it connects to the core values. The number of definitions produced equals twenty (Total time - 2 minutes).

2 - Group members are placed in pairs at each table (2 pairs per table). Each member of each pair is given two minutes to explain to their pair partner how they define relationships. After each group member has used their two minutes to define relationships, they are both given one minute to choose one answer between the two. The total number of definitions decreases to ten (Total time - 5 minutes).

4 - Group members share their definitions with all four members of their table group. (Four definitions shared out). Next, all four members of the group must agree on one definition per table to share out with

the entire room. The outcome of definitions now equals five (Total time - 5 minutes).

After each round, responses are curated and displayed for all to see (whiteboard, chart paper, google document, etc.) In this example, the number of definitions for the word relationships went from 20 to 10 to 5, with every person having a voice in deciding the best definitions.

Next, we would continue to repeat the same procedure until the original number of twenty definitions was down to one definition for relationships (or whatever number is agreed upon prior, depending on the number of responses the team is trying to generate).

Round two would begin by displaying the five definitions and then starting the 1 - 2 - 4 framework again.

1 - Group members are provided independent time to decide which of the five definitions they select as their #1 choice (1 minute).

2 - Group members are placed in pairs again at each table and given two minutes each to explain the reason for their choice. Once again, after four minutes they are given one additional minute to decide on their final choice together between their two options. (5 minutes.

4 - Group members all share their choice and, as a table group, must decide on one final definition for their table and share it with the entire room (5 minutes).

During round two, responses are curated and displayed again for all to see.

Whether you choose to use this framework or another framework, the reason for doing so should be to ensure each member of the team is given a voice. Too often it is the individual voice that is missing from the process, leaving it up to a select few to influence the outcome, and ultimately leaving people feeling like they didn't have a say in the decision. When this happens at building or district-level meetings, it can be a morale killer and create a natural undercurrent of unease or unrest. When it happens at the classroom level, the failures are often seen in academic and performance assessments because we thought that all students were involved, when, in reality, our superficial efforts at eliciting responses fooled us and left us disappointed in our results.

References:

Sinek, Simon. *Start with Why: How Great Leaders Inspire Everyone to Take Action.* Portfolio; Reprint Edition, 2011.

Pulver. 2017, May 4. Be a Mr. Jensen[Video]. YouTube. https://www.youtube.com/watch?v=4p5286T_kn0&t=4s&ab_channel=ClintPulver

Morgado P, Cerquiera, JJ. 2018. Chronic stress affects motivation. Editorial: The Impact of Stress on Cognition and Motivation. Front. Behav. Neurosci. 12:326. doi: 10.3389/fnbeh.2018.00326

Bains. 2018. Being in close contact with stressed people increases your stress levels.

Maier, et al. 2015. Stress impairs self control.

Yuen et al. 2012. Stress impairs memory.

Kim, et al. 2015. The hippocampus (the part of the brain that processes memory) is smaller in those with chronic stress.

Zoccola, et al. 2013. Dwelling on stressful events increases inflammation in the body.

Ressler KJ. 2010. The amygdala part of the brain that modulates the fear response, is highly activated during times of stress. Amygdala activity, fear, and anxiety: modulation by stress. Biol Psychiatry. 67(12):1117–1119. doi:10.1016/j.biopsych.2010.04.027)

Reflect AND
RECALIBRATE

(Use the following space for reflective notes)

CHAPTER 3

Premise 2: Cultivate a Community of Leaders

We've been leading past people.
We need to lead alongside them.

The story goes that two lumberjacks–an older one and a younger one–were both known for their expertise and speed. Both were fearless lumberjacks and could clear big trees swiftly out of a forest. One day the younger man challenged the older one to a contest to see who could cut down the most trees in a day.

The next day the contest began and both men set out with their axes and went to work. The younger man began in earnest chopping down one tree after another without stopping. One tree after the other fell, both men using their skill with an axe to cut down many trees. About midday, the younger man noticed that the older lumberjack chopped trees for about an hour and then took a fifteen-minute break. He laughed that the older man could not keep up with him, needing that break to rest.

At the end of the day when the felled trees were counted, the older lumberjack had chopped down one-third more trees than the younger lumberjack. Puzzled, the younger lumberjack asked the older, "How could you, taking a break every hour, cut down more trees than I did cutting nonstop all day?"

The older lumberjack responded, "Because when I stopped and you thought I was taking a break, I was actually sharpening my axe."

How many of us are trying to teach and lead with dull axes? How many of us are carrying those dull axes into the school building alone? This second premise of *Culturize* reminds us that everyone can lead, and effective leaders cultivate a community of leaders to help lead the campus. When we as a community sharpen our axes together, rather than compete against one another, and give each other permission to help us live our collective commitments as was described at the end of the last chapter, we recalibrate an environment in which all members of the school community look forward to coming to school every day ready to learn.

Sense of Belonging

Show me a school with a healthy culture and chances are, they have been successful in creating a greater sense of belonging for the people who walk through the school doors each day–students, families, staff, and guests alike. Teachers are intentional in taking time to get to know their students on a personal level. They engage them with a smile on their face. They ask questions. They give them opportunities to talk about their experiences and then listen with the sincere intent of wanting to understand those experiences. Teachers realize that going through these stages of discovery allows students to share their experiences and bring value to who they are. When we deny our students, staff, and families these experiences and don't take time to listen to and appreciate their stories, we can bring harm to them by devaluing their worth.

An inviting school has likely recalibrated as a staff and agreed through their collective commitments how they will behave when they greet a guest, a new student, a family, a guest teacher, and one another. More importantly, they hold each other accountable to live those commitments. School and district leaders carry the same responsibility of ensuring they bring the same level of commitment and create a sense of belonging for all students, teachers, principals, guests, and families. They must be intentional in connecting to those with whom they are closest. They carry the additional responsibilities of Core Principle 2, to make sure they are modeling the behaviors they want their colleagues to emulate. They never lose sight of the fact that the key to their success and the success of the school community lies in their ability to encourage, invite, support, and inspire others to want to lead with them. By partnering with all stakeholders and sharpening their axes together, they can lead alongside them, rather than past them.

It's Not About the Direction, Rather the Redirection

Weakness in leadership will eventually result in a weakened culture. Effective leaders are keenly aware of this. Therefore, they don't put a spotlight on people's shortcomings. Instead, they focus on their talents to build their confidence so they, in turn, can do the same for others. They seek to understand people's goals and then place those goals on a shelf where they can reach them. If their people need a step stool or a ladder, then they will be less likely to achieve the goal. Frequently, principals and superintendents who are teetering on burnout, find themselves trying to do too much on their own and have convinced themselves that they are the only ones who either can do the work, will do the work, or are worried that they will lose their team if they ask them to do one more thing. This becomes

> Weakness in leadership will eventually result in a weakened culture.

even more common among leaders who are working in smaller schools, rural schools, and isolated districts. If you are approaching the boundary line of isolation and burnout and worry about your ability to function productively due to limited resources, it may be beneficial to recalibrate your approach and seek new ways to leverage the talents of others. Staff shortages are a real challenge many schools and district leaders have faced, even more so during this pandemic.

One challenge you may struggle with that I alluded to above is asking others to do more when they have already been burdened with so much. Close your eyes for a moment and reframe it. You are not assigning or delegating more tasks or work, you are partnering with your staff, colleagues, and teammates and leaning into one another. Our work is not about the direction, but rather the redirection, and we are going to have to redirect our resources and partner with them to get a better result. When we sharpen our axes together rather than in isolation, it can create an uplifting feeling of joy, a revelation that, together, we can accomplish more than we thought possible, and not be exhausted. Your team needs a win to keep hope alive, a hope for a better result. My experience has shown me that depleted people can become re-energized quickly when they see their efforts produce results. When those results are achieved together, it catapults your team to new heights, bringing about a surge of newfound energy and a belief they can do it all over again.

Grow Your Office Teams

In our work with school and district leaders, we have witnessed effective leaders who grow and develop their teams by leaning into their teams to help them lead. Too many attempts to travel the leadership road alone and you can quickly find yourself leading from an empty tank. I took this road one too many times throughout my career and it cost me dearly. Many of us don't see it at the moment, but we carry that empty tank home with us as well, leaving us depleted with little to give to our own families. Remember the core begins with you, with your significant others in that inner ring.

John was one of those superintendents who worked on his team, starting with his administrative assistant. Wendy had worked for several superintendents over the years. This was John's second year in his position, and he learned early on that Wendy had an uncanny ability to connect with people and he leaned into her to help him understand the history of the community and how "things" had been done before his arrival. Wendy also saw things and heard things most didn't, and more importantly, people trusted her as a confidant, even though they knew she was loyal to John. He knew that she was critical to his success. She not only helped him keep his eye on the big picture, but she also kept him focused on the small details. Neglecting small details can derail us quickly and keep us from accomplishing our goals.

In my observations of John, I learned that he would meet with Wendy each morning for a fifteen-minute meeting to go over the day's calendar. The demands of the job and the pacing of each day are enough to make our heads spin in circles, so we need to ensure we are on time getting from location A to location B. Effective leaders know the challenges of managing a complex conversation with an employee who shows up late regularly and modeling the same poor behaviors is not going to bode well when it comes time to have that conversation. The short, but valuable, time together allowed them both to catch up on the previous day's work, update each other on conversations they engaged in with staff, discuss calls and meetings for the day, and communicate timelines that needed to be met.

The role of the administrative assistant is critical to the success of all campus leaders, yet is one that is often underutilized. Meeting daily with members of your office team and/or administrative team is critical to your success. Talking throughout the day as you cross paths with so many people, all the while with ten other things on your mind is not the same and will not produce the results you need to perform at a high level. We live and work in a hyper-critical world that no longer allows free passes on missed calls, meetings, observations, events, etc. For every missed obligation, your credit rating drops, and eventually, you will be seen as unorganized and undependable, and we cannot afford for that to happen to our leaders. So, recalibrate and get back to meeting daily with your office partner(s) to achieve a better outcome.

To Delegate or Not to Delegate?

Have you ever delegated a task to someone only to be disappointed in the result? I recall having experienced it many times throughout my career. And each time it happened, I grew more frustrated with my staff to the point I complained about them, quit asking them, and, worse yet, labeled them at times.

Have you ever not delegated a task to someone because you convinced yourself that by the time you explained it to them, you could have already done it yourself? Too much hassle to explain it when I can just do it myself, and quicker and better, my ego would often remind me. And it was that same ego that would catch me, and then trap me in those moments of feeling overwhelmed, exhausted, and then wearing that exhaustion as a badge of honor because of all the things I had to do, and then turning around and complaining about it at the same time.

This would all change for me after complaining to Jim about an experience I had with one of our staff members who I had asked to serve as a game manager for a volleyball game. I met with Pam and asked her if she was interested in covering the event for me the following Thursday. She seemed excited and was looking for ways to supplement her income and she saw this as an opportunity to pick up some extra hours. I described in detail what she would need to do that evening as she quickly scrambled to write everything down. When I was done talking, I asked her if she had any questions, to which she quickly replied, "No, I think I got it all." I recall telling my secretary at the time how excited I was about Pam covering for me and that, eventually, this would give me some additional support I had been looking for. That evening, I sent her a quick text to see how things were going and she assured me that everything was going well.

On Friday morning, my secretary walked into my office and told me that Pam had called in a panic because the gate and concession monies were missing. She had taken the money home with her, and she believed that someone had stolen it from her car. "What!?" I erupted. Did she take the money home with her? What was she thinking? I specifically told her to call Tom (our school officer) at the end of the night and have him place it in the safe. How much money are we talking about?" I asked?

"I'm afraid it's around $1500," my secretary explained. At that moment, I was angry and sick to my stomach.

The day would go from bad to worse as I received additional complaints throughout the day, including the head of officials, my custodians, parents, and my booster club president. By the end of the day, I was convinced I would never allow anyone to ever manage a game for me again. Thank goodness for Jim who helped me reframe my thinking and see it differently. Pam had done her best. She certainly didn't want to lose that money. She didn't want the stress that she endured as she worried about the consequences that would follow. And she certainly didn't want to disappoint me. As upset as I was at the time for the "extra" work that this situation created, I felt bad for Pam. As time passed, I began to learn more about how leaders delegated and built capacity. Eventually, I would create a framework to help me and, more importantly, help others experience success and build confidence in their ability to perform their responsibilities at a high level. Here is a short explanation of each step:

1. **Tell - CLARITY**: Be clear in your expectations and what you are asking others to do.
2. **Show - MODEL**: Once you've clearly explained to the individual what you need them to do, provide a model by allowing them to observe you do what you are asking them to do.
3. **Observe - EXPECTATIONS**: By observing the individual, you can see for yourself where they are not meeting your expectations and you can help fill in the gaps.
4. **Feedback - QUESTIONS**: This is the time for questions and providing feedback. This begins the coaching cycle, as both people are invested in sharing feedback, asking clarifying expectations, and modeling how things should be done. This is the most critical step for building confidence. This may result in additional opportunities for observation.
5. **Replicate - CAPACITY**: This is the stage at which capacity is built and you allow the student to become the teacher, having them follow the same framework you previously worked through together. You delegate to them not merely tasks, but opportunities to continue to grow and develop the capacity of others.

The framework pictured below has been tweaked over the years and continues to serve as a guide to educators at the classroom, building, and district levels alike, supporting teachers, principals, and district office administrators to bring their best selves to others as they continue to coach and replicate future leaders across the system.

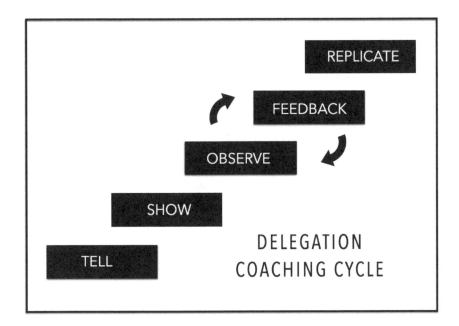

Trade the Time

In case you are wondering whatever happened to Pam regarding the money being stolen, well, I am happy to inform you that everything worked out. The money was recovered. I still carry the lessons I learned from that experience. I often share this story when I am presenting or working with leaders. They understand when I reframe the situation, realizing that Pam was never the issue; I was. It was just easier for me to blame Pam than it was to look at myself. Had I followed this framework, I can confidently say it would have ended differently and saved all of us a lot of time, stress, and grief. Teachers can fall into the same trap as well, at times blaming students for their lack of follow through or quality of work and the district office can look to place blame on building-level administrators and teachers when their expectations are not met. It is hard for teachers to see it and equally hard for district leaders to see it. We all are susceptible to seeing unpleasant events from only one perspective.

Rarely will someone disagree with the idea that following this framework would yield better results. However, many leaders still fail to implement a framework with regularity, even though they know it works. Why, do you ask? The most common response is they don't have time. What they fail to see is that they do. They just need to reframe it and change it from *having the time* to *trading the time*.

When we fail to invest in people on the front end by not taking the necessary time to tell, show, observe, provide feedback, and replicate to build capacity, we lose time on the back end. I may have convinced myself I didn't have time to go through the proper delegation steps with Pam, but that went by the wayside after several phone calls and meetings with the head of officials, my custodians, parents, and my booster club president. The need to follow up with more issues that I created when I failed to invest time on the front end began with me. Either way, we will put in the time. We just have to ask ourselves when and where we want to place that time. Too often we see time as a barrier to our success when, in actuality, time is our biggest ally.

I've learned to avoid the back end because it is often stressful, causing me to worry or lose sleep due to the nature of the conversation that must take place and that has the potential to go sideways rather quickly. I prefer the front end because it aligns with Core Value 1 of *Culturize*: Invest time in people. When I am intentional and invest time in people, it takes me back to the interview chair and reminds me of what I said I would do for others if given the opportunity. Well, I was given the opportunity and I want to be the person I said I would be. To do so, I needed to reframe it—trade time to save time.

Empower Your Building Leadership Team

I am convinced that building leadership capacity is the key to a long successful tenure for any principal. Sometimes leadership fails. When that happens, we need to count on our staff to get us through. Empowering a community of leaders to help you lead can be a game-changer for any building leader. The talent is on your staff to take your school to the next level.

To begin, as suggested earlier when working with your secretary or admin assistant, recommit to also meeting with your building leadership team regularly to cultivate a high-performing team to help you lead. You will need to reflect on and create a process for building your leadership team, including the criteria for selection. You must communicate to the entire staff that anyone can express interest but that you will have the final say based on the criteria you have shared out, including a final interview process should you have multiple people express interest. I recommend reconvening all members of your current team (if applicable) and communicating expectations to the team, including their role, responsibilities, calendar of meeting dates, etc. You may also want to elicit their input regarding ideas they may have for strengthening the leadership team using the 1 -2 - 4 Framework to assist you. After gathering feedback from your team, ask your secretary to help you create a schedule, so members are clear on the time commitment and the purpose of the leadership team.

One thing to avoid is calling on the same staff members repeatedly to carry the workload. When we identify those people on our staff who have talent, we can easily begin to rely on the same people over and over. Because these staff members are highly valued, go-getters, and are seen as team players, it will be hard for them to say no to someone like you who they like and respect. Unfortunately, over time, this can lead to fatigue, burnout, and eventually, grow into resentment if they feel that the workload is not being spread out evenly among all staff members. Some will begin to keep score even though that is not their nature to do. Work with your secretary to create a process whereby you are tracking requests and act intentionally to empower others on your staff, beyond the leadership team, to assist you in moving the school forward.

Every Meeting Ever?

Remind me again. What was the class you took in principal school that taught you how to run an effective meeting? Yeah, I don't recall that class either. We get a phone call, letting us know we have the job. We are as excited as a teenager whose parents are going away for the weekend (hope that didn't just make you change your vacation plans). We accept the position. We visit the school and check out our office space. And then it hits us. Crap! I've got an opening faculty meeting to prepare for. Moreover, Casas just shared that I need to hold regular meetings with my secretary, office staff, and my building leadership team to create a community of leaders. What? When? How?

I don't know what the exact number is, but I would love to see a study conducted on the amount of time that educators spend in meetings every month. Even without a qualified study, I know that the minutes endured in offices, classrooms, conference rooms, and other large spaces where we come together as a team or faculty, is time that could be repurposed differently to improve morale and create a healthier environment for all students and staff. Data from the cultural assessments that we conduct as part of our coaching work indicates that teachers often see meetings as a waste of time. In our defense of building and campus leaders, I already shared that no class taught us how to run an effective meeting. Ironically, principals express the same sentiment when it comes to their district-wide leadership meetings, but, hey, before we get too critical, remember, that class doesn't exist for superintendents, either. Teachers struggle, too. If there was no class in admin school to help us navigate meetings effectively, we can all but guarantee our teachers didn't find that class in the course guidebook in college either.

Visit a school on any given day between the hours of 7:00 a.m. and 5:00 p.m. and beyond, and you will be sure to find educators in meetings trying to plan a lesson, identify standards, work on proficiency scales, resolve an issue, placate a parent, discuss strategies for a student with special needs, plan for an event, figure out a budget item issue, or prepare for yet another meeting. Hours and hours and yet no formal training or framework to help guide our people.

If you have ever seen the YouTube video, entitled, *Every Meeting Ever*, (Tripp and Tyler, 2014) you may be able to relate to the actors who portray the frustrations that many educators face during meetings. At one time or another, we have all encountered one of these characters and in some instances, we may have been these characters: *The Dominator, The Time Nazi, Never on Time Guy, Nancy the Negator, Ol' Thin Skin, Bad Idea Man* and, finally, the *Rambler*, who seems to just go on and on, talking in circles and leaving the others wondering what the heck is he talking about?

Pause and reflect for a moment and ask yourself how often are you walking out of a meeting feeling proud of the work that was completed? Feeling like you connected with some members of the team on a more personal level? Did you leave the meeting looking forward to the next meeting? Are you leaving meetings feeling inspired, like you and the team could accomplish anything you set your minds to? Or when was the last time you left a meeting and felt like it was a waste of time because you didn't understand why you had to meet to get the same information you could have gotten in an email, or you left the meeting and still weren't clear what the purpose of the meeting was? Finally, when was the last time you attended a meeting and felt like you couldn't share what was on your mind because you either thought it wouldn't matter or you didn't feel like you could speak openly about your true feelings without offending someone?

The content above and the content I talk about in my presentations or write about in my books all come from educators like you who are frustrated with the average that exists in their workplace. If the descriptions above are not your experience, I am sincerely happy for you, but sadly, your experiences are not the standard in all schools across the country. You are the exception. I hope to support all of you to create a better standard so we can recalibrate a healthier culture across all levels to impact the entire system in a positive way to bring about sustainable change. Consider including each step of the following protocol as part of your meetings:

- **Connections**: See yourself as a community builder. Every time you bring a group of people together it is an opportunity to build community. Remember, you can't outsource relationships to someone else. High-performing teams are highly-connected teams. Give your people time to get to know one another on a more personal level.
- **Purpose**: People need to know why they are meeting. What is the overarching reason for holding this meeting? Is it clear? Has it been communicated?
- **Process**: The most important component of any process is voice. People need more than a seat at the table. If you want people to invest and contribute to the meeting in a positive way, then make certain you give them a voice at the table.
- **Deliverables**: What are the participants walking away with from the meeting? Whatever it is, do they see the value in it? Will it help them in some way? If not, you run the danger of them seeing the meeting as a waste of time.
- **Summary**: This one goes hand-in-hand with the deliverables. Make sure before they leave the room, you make time to summarize the deliverables, so they see the value in the meeting. If there are tasks to be completed before the next meeting, be sure to review what they are and who will complete them.

Examine the meeting protocol closely. What does it remind you of? It looks similar to a lesson plan. When districts place an emphasis on developing processes, protocols, and frameworks, and then communicate those expectations and model them across the district, then we begin to see how each level is provided the necessary tools to help support them in their quest to align themselves within the system.

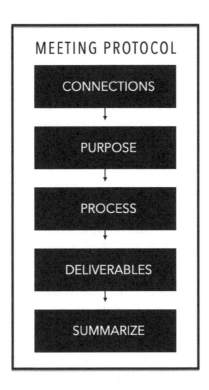

80/20 Equals Consensus...But Not Commitment

You are now equipped with a meeting protocol to help you continue to grow and develop as an educator. After all, we are in the teaching and learning profession, so we must continue to model what it means to be a learner if we are going to expect our students to learn each day they come to school. Think Core Value 2: We don't ask others to do what we are not willing to do ourselves. A gentle reminder–you need not use the protocol I provided, but my hope is that you will better understand the need for *some* protocol if you are aiming for a better result and aspire to nudge the morale barometer further into the positive range. However, danger still lurks around the corner, and we must be careful not to move too quickly. Other factors can swiftly find their way into the mix which can cause disruption, interfering with the results we hoped for.

I was struggling—to say the least. It was my second year as a principal, and I had been charged by my superintendent to implement a new initiative that would require every student in my building to have an ISP (Individualized Success Plan). These plans were to include both an academic and behavioral component. Ironically, I had been vocal in our administrative meetings during my first year as a principal about the need for such a plan to support our students.

I was so excited when it was announced over the summer entering that second year that we would be expected to put this plan into place. I could hardly wait. I had all these thoughts and ideas running through my head and I had notes written down describing how I would make this work. I worked diligently that July to have everything ready to go in time for the opening of school. When I introduced the plan at the beginning-of-the-year faculty meeting, I assured everyone that this would be great for all our students. I gave what I thought was a powerful message on why I thought we needed to do this, told them not to worry, and that more details would follow in the coming days. The fact that there were only a couple of questions from the staff members in attendance left me feeling confident that this would be a game changer for the students we served.

It was a game changer all right, but not the kind I had envisioned. Within a couple of weeks, I was receiving pushback from many on our staff, including my best teachers who I was convinced would trust me and be on board. I could not understand why they weren't buying in. I was so disappointed, frustrated, and, quite frankly, angry at them.

Rather than go back and reflect on my practices, I chose to blame them. How could they not see that this was the right thing to do for our students?

As we near the halfway point of this book, I hope you can see what I was not able to see at the time. The meeting protocol that I've provided has embedded a step that all healthy cultures practice to ensure a better outcome: the process step. As I noted in the previous section, the most important component of any process is deliberately giving everyone a voice at the table to promote investment and engagement.

More than two decades later I can now look back on those early years and let out a smile. Although I know I will never figure it all out, I can at least see where I fell short; where I mismanaged it all. As I worked through those summer months during my second-year prepping for the change in the ISP, I bypassed giving people a voice in the vision planning. I created the vision on my own because that is what I had been asked to do. I never contemplated empowering our staff members to have a say in that vision.

It's much clearer now. It just wasn't clear to me then. And clarity is vital if you aim to implement positive change effectively. However, so is the process. A common problem we see in schools today is a weak process for building consensus or a lack of process altogether.

When was the last time you felt it was important to build consensus to move forward, but then found yourself moving forward anyway because you couldn't come to a consensus and get everyone to agree and land on that 80-20 rule? You've heard of it, right? Get 80% of your staff to get on the bus or the bus will leave without them. The problem with this approach is that the 20% who don't get on will likely not be committed, and this gap will create a division between them and the 80% who came to a consensus and are completely invested.

Building a consensus requires us as leaders to develop a disciplined, systematic process for getting as many members of the team on the bus and inspiring them to invest in what we are trying to accomplish. One simple recalibration on our part can lead to a better outcome for our overall culture. For one, a 10% increase in consensus because we used a more effective process gives us a better result and reduces the division among the staff, thereby improving morale. Secondly, herein lies an opportunity for us to incorporate the Power of Why x 3 Framework to help us understand the "why" of those who chose not to join the others on the consensus bus. Third, we must continue to find ways to support, invest in, and influence those staff members who are not in agreement with the initiative, so they do not feel like outliers and find themselves isolated from the majority.

One simple, yet intentional and powerful protocol is called *Fist-to-Five Consensus Protocol*. To follow this protocol, you first must explain the value system as follows:

5: All In
4: In Agreement
3: On the Fence
2: Not Convinced
1: Unlikely
0 (Fist): Cannot Support.

Transparency is vital. Before moving forward with a new idea, initiative, or decision, each member of the team visibly shares out a number based on their level of support. Everyone can see where everyone stands. Next steps and considerations include the following:

- Investment approval to move forward requires all members to vote with a score of 4 or 5 for consensus to be reached, or the discussion continues.
- The leader facilitates discussion by allowing members of the team to explain their voting levels. Team members voting in

the 4-5 range are responsible for moving all members of the team to their level through persuasive conversation. When the conversation comes to an end, leaders request a new *Fist to Five* vote. The leader then asks the remaining members who are not at a 4-5 level what it would take to move them to that level for approval. The discussion begins again until the leader calls for a new vote.

+ If we follow the 80-20 rule, then consensus is defined when 80% of all members of the team reach a 4-5 level of agreement. If this cannot be reached, then the decision is tabled and the process begins again.

+ The 20% who were not in agreement continue to receive full support from the administration to cultivate a culture where healthy dissension is supported.

I believe that moving forward with anything less than 100% consensus has great potential to lead to divisions within the culture if we are not careful. We also know that we will not always get 100% investment. However, by implementing a process in which every voice matters and dialogue is encouraged, supported, and valued, leaders can better understand why some people struggle to offer their full support and, more importantly, they minimize divisions. There is a tremendous benefit for classroom cultures as well when teachers infuse the *Fist-to-Five Consensus Protocol* or another process that values students' voices. This leads to fewer incidents in classrooms that promote divisions among students, especially those that are perpetuated by a lack of dialogue or understanding.

The more we model and teach fair and transparent processes, the more likely we are to recalibrate a healthier culture of dialogue and trust, a culture in which everyone can continue to move towards a commitment to get on the bus.

Perimeter Leadership vs. Inner Leadership

Have you ever encountered a person who, after you spend any amount of time with them, makes you feel like the most important person in the world? These individuals have a certain aura about them that makes you want to stay in their space for as long as possible because of their unique ability to uplift others. The opposite is also true. These people appear to serve one purpose and one purpose only—to make us feel icky. At one time or another, we have all experienced the burden of these toxic people. They are often negative, bitter, and cynical. At times they can be arrogant, disruptive, and rarely contribute anything of value to the team. Truthfully speaking, they can be a heavy load to bear.

In the opening chapter, I touched on my frustrations with a teacher who I felt wasn't good for kids. Frankly, I wasn't sure how to address the dozens of complaints that I received from students, families, and colleagues regarding his treatment of others. There were countless complaints from his peers regarding his negative gossip about students, even to the point of advising some of his teammates which students to avoid. Counselors would come to me privately, sharing that he was putting pressure on them to remove students from his class who he felt were not "honors" material. Special education teachers were fed up with him because he wouldn't follow the individualized education plan and provide accommodations for certain students. No one was immune. It wasn't uncommon to receive double-digit requests from parents every year for a teacher change. Students reported incidents of unfair treatment and we, as an administrative team, complained about the number of students he was sending out of the classroom. Each year, I found myself becoming increasingly frustrated, to the point that I tagged him with a not-so-kind label. I avoided him as much as possible, blamed him for the struggles of many of our students, and eventually, I gave up on him. I was officially on the perimeter.

In my daily work as a Leadership Coach, it is common for me to observe students, teachers, and administrators leading from the perimeter. I hear it in their comments and see it in their behavior. I don't judge them for it; after all, that would be hypocritical of me since I led from there for many years. My guess is if I walked into your classroom or school, I might find some of you leading from out there as well. Often, you and others don't see it; hence, my role is to point it out, the same way Jim pointed it out to me.

I was at my wit's end with this teacher and Jim helped me approach it differently. Here is what he shared with me that helped me reframe it:

1.   It wasn't my job to change him, it was my job to change me.
2.   Quit trying to fix and solve all the issues and focus on becoming a better version of yourself to get a better result.
3.   When he was hired, he didn't think or behave that way. He became that way. Believe you can help him find his way back.
4.   If he came to you and was struggling with a student, what advice would you give him? Now ask yourself: Are you modeling what you would ask him to do?
5.   Flip it. Don't point the finger at him. Start with your inner self. You may not see it, but in some way(s) you are contributing to this issue, so keep looking inward.

Admittedly, my initial meeting with this teacher was not great, but I did feel better, especially about the way I managed myself. I recall at the time feeling more positive and sharing the experience with my administrative team. More importantly, it lit a fire under me because it reminded me of what I said when I sat in the interview chair, how I wanted to build relationships with my students and staff, how I wanted to be their champion, and how I wanted to inspire them to be more and do more than they ever thought possible.

If you are still hanging in there with me and reading along, you know how this ends—with the development of the Core Principles of *Culturize*. However, what you don't know is that even though I had a framework to support me, I still encountered many ups and downs throughout my entire twenty-two years as a school leader. I couldn't just flip the switch and change overnight after behaving a certain way for so many years, but I could continue to commit to staying the course. I share this with you to remind you that we are all a work in progress, that we are not perfect beings. There are no perfect processes or frameworks that can or will solve all your problems, but they almost always ensure a better result. More importantly, you become better. You just have to keep reframing it, stay away from the perimeter, and start with your inner self.

So how would I advise we deal with negative parents, teachers, and administrators today? Using the core values of *Culturize*, let's do our best to stay off the perimeter and lead with these values in the following ways: For the teacher who has lost his way, try seeing it as more of a leadership issue and less of a teacher issue. He needs a champion. Don't quit on him and invest more time to understand his story and his experiences, and listen to how he landed in the spot where he stands today. Two, be a *Merchant of Hope*. Remember that he wants to be great at what he does, and believe that you can help him find his way back to the same person he was when he sat in that interview chair. Three, make sure you change your language and don't see it as "dealing" with him, but rather "partnering" with him so his experience with you is so positive, that he will *Carry the Banner* for you when he shares that experience with others because you treated him with dignity and compassion. Finally, hold him to the highest of standards. *Expect Excellence* from him and do not allow him to opt-out or fall back to average. Be clear in your expectations of him, but also be sure to provide him the necessary support, guidance, resources, and time to become the best version of himself.

Teachers can also find themselves inching towards the perimeter when we become frustrated with certain student behaviors. Do your best to hold back and find your inner leadership. Begin to see students who demonstrate a reluctance to learn or whose behaviors do not meet your expectations from an inner perspective. Eventually, you will encounter students who put their heads on the desk and appear to be unmotivated and refuse to do the work. Other students will communicate through their words or body language that they don't care, and others will challenge your authority and sometimes even cross the line into disrespect. These students need your best as well. Reframe it, don't quit on them, invest time to listen to their story, maintain high expectations, but approach the conversation and your actions so when the conversation is over, they actually carry the banner for you. Finally, regardless of their initial response, believe all students want to be successful and when one pushes back, reframe it by reminding yourself that perhaps they just aren't ready to trust you and let you in at that moment, but maybe they will be tomorrow.

I feel compelled to tell you that this will not be easy. Flipping the switch will not come naturally in some cases, just like it didn't come easy to me. Your first reaction might be to run towards the outer edges of the perimeter and blame the student or administration. Or maybe you will point the finger at your colleague or the parent(s), or their previous school for their behavior and/or the lack of support that you are getting in having to "deal" with this student. Do your best to resist the urge to run to the perimeter. It is okay if you need to work from a sprint to a run, to a jog, to a walk, to standing still. Everything worth doing takes time and will not

> Even the most challenging students and staff need us to believe in them. Believe that they care. Believe that they can. Believe that they will.

happen overnight. As you progress through each of these stages, you will begin to reap the rewards of your efforts in the way your students and colleagues see you and respond to you. Even the most challenging students and staff need us to believe in them. Believe that they care. Believe that they can. Believe that they will.

Managing Complex Conversations

Let's take a deeper dive into my conversation with the teacher above who, regrettably, I labeled a s*#%ty teacher. There is a good chance that at one time or another, you have fallen into the trap of mismanaging a conversation. I cannot even begin to tell you how many times I found myself throughout my career looking for a way out of a conversation after it went sideways on me. It still happens now and then but definitely with less frequency and less intensity. As I have stated before, I believe it is because I have not only learned from my mistakes, but I have changed the way I approach and manage these conversations that have helped me achieve a better result. In my work with schools today, I strive to help educators see that they won't always get it right and that is okay as long as they continue to pull back from the perimeter (placing blame on students) and work on their inner core (focus on themselves). We cannot continue to complain about the way students are behaving, yet fail to recognize that we, as adults, need to work on our self-management as well, especially if we want to see improvement in our classroom, hallway, cafeteria, playground, and overall campus culture. As we have learned, a poor process is usually a magnet for a poor result.

> A poor process is usually a magnet for a poor result.

Here is a framework that I created to support teachers and leaders to ensure they use "softer language" when managing complex conversations with students, teachers, and families. A framework is a critical tool to not only assist leaders in holding ourselves accountable for modeling the behaviors we want others to emulate, but it also serves as a teaching tool to support our teachers when they must navigate delicate conversations with students and parents. Once again, I am not suggesting that you use this particular framework, but I strongly believe you should create (and utilize) a framework of some type to keep you steady, consistent, and focused, and to ensure that you treat students and staff in a way that aligns with a set of core values, resulting in a healthy and positive culture in which people feel valued and respected:

1. **Validation:** Start with a sincere question or comment to check how they are currently feeling. Examples include: "How are you doing?" "Are you feeling okay?" "I am worried about you." "You seem upset." "Is everything okay?" The key is in your response because if we cared enough to ask, then we should accept the response, regardless of how kind, harsh, or dismissive it is. In other words, validate their feelings and thank them for trusting you with their feelings.

2. **Inquiry:** Follow up with probing questions. I recommend a minimum of 3-5 questions to better understand the root problem. Moving too quickly or not having yet developed the skills to comprehend the complexities of the behavior can result in us misdiagnosing the "real issue," potentially making things more complex for us. This also helps us avoid perimeter thinking.

3. **Expectations:** Brene Brown states that "Clear is kind. Unclear is unkind." (Brown, 2018, p. 68.) We must listen, validate, and ask questions to better understand, but it is also important that we clarify our expectations. We must not allow people to opt-out or behave in ways that are contrary to our expectations. Behavior equals culture and the worst behavior we allow or tolerate will eventually define our actual culture.

4. **Process Time:** Once expectations have been stated, this is the time to acknowledge they may need some time to process the conversation. Thank them for any positives they may have demonstrated during the conversation, thank them for allowing you to share your expectations, and then give them time to reflect.

5. **Close the Circle:** Be sure to circle back later in the day or the next day to check on them to see how they are feeling about the conversation and assure them that you are sincere in your concern and offer of support.

Every conversation is different, and we can never predict how it will go. That being said, we should not ignore the fact that when we are intentional in reframing the way we see things and do things, our thinking begins to influence the way we behave, and we find ourselves well on our way to becoming more effective in our work and bringing our perimeter thinking back to our inner core to recalibrate our values and our behavior.

MANAGING COMPLEX CONVERSATIONS

Validation

Inquiry

Expectations

Process Time

Close the Circle

Developing the confidence to manage complex conversations takes time. I believe it is the most difficult skill to develop, primarily because it is our nature to avoid conversations that feel or appear confrontational. This reason alone should convince us of the importance of packing as many tools as possible into our toolbox to serve as a reminder that we are talking about a specific skill, and skills can only be developed when we practice them. Below are a few more items to consider as you continue to seek additional ways to manage conversations more effectively:

1. **Re-Focus on the Emotion:** One way to better manage a conversation is to slow down our response time and focus on the emotion of the other individual. This may contradict what we have heard in the past about listening to the words being spoken, but to get the results we want and not end up on the perimeter, it was clear we would need to reframe it, and immediately, we experienced better results with students, teachers, and leaders. When we pay more attention to the words, we tend to look for places where we can argue and place blame rather than see the hurt and pain others are expressing.

2. **Relationships First:** Without a doubt, it is more challenging to manage a complex conversation with someone when a prior meaningful relationship has not been established. So the next time you are contemplating having a conversation with a student who is not meeting expectations, ask yourself how much time you have invested in this person to know their story. Hold off on a conversation (if possible) or consider delegating the conversation to someone else who may have a better relationship with this person. If this is not an option, tread lightly.

3. **Reflection Before Reaction:** I believe it is difficult to grow as teachers and leaders when we fail to take time to reflect. We cannot ignore our role in leading the way in this arena. Doing so would risk our credibility with students since we expect

them to reflect and learn daily. Slowing down our response time helps us regulate our emotions, the same skill we expect our students to develop and exhibit.

4. **Remember Your Inner Voice:** Oftentimes we only hear the voices *around* us when we should be paying just as much attention to the voice *within* us. Always remember that your inner voice matters, too.

5. **Release Your Power:** Just because we have the power to make a final decision doesn't translate to us always being right. In these moments we must control our need to be right so that it doesn't jeopardize our credibility by taking away someone's insight and voice.

Using a framework for managing complex conversations permits us to acknowledge that we all need assistance now and then when it comes to holding people to a higher standard for their performance. These tools also protect us and help keep us anchored to our core values during stressful situations, so the conversation is less likely to go off the rails, thereby giving us a better result. Finally, it provides a model for us and others when we use a framework to ensure that our message is not lost in translation by the way we managed the conversation; rather, it allows us to reframe things in a way that brings the best version of ourselves to the conversation.

References:

Tripp and Tyler, 2014, November 5. Every Meeting Ever[Video]. YouTube. https://www.youtube.com/watch?v=K7agjXFFQJU&ab_channel=TrippandTyler

Brown, Brene (2018). Dare to Lead. Random House.

Reflect AND RECALIBRATE

(Use the following space for reflective notes)

CHAPTER 4

Premise 3: See the Culture Through the Eyes of Others

It's easy to ignore the resistors. Pay close attention to what they have to say. Everyone's voice and perspective matters.

If you have ever watched an episode of Ted Lasso, you know the show's wonderful heart and underlying messages are incredibly refreshing and memorable. In one scene, Coach Ted Lasso (Why You Laughing?, 2020), played by Jason Sudeikis, an alum of *Saturday Night Live*, is challenged to a dart game by the show's villain, Rupert Mannion, former owner of the soccer team that Ted now coaches. It is clear that Rupert, a seasoned dart player, is not fond of Ted and wants to show off to the guests by humiliating Ted. Of all the show's inspiring messages, this one scene, in particular, stood out to me more than any other scene.

As Ted prepares to throw his first dart, he states, "You know, Rupert. Guys have underestimated me my entire life and for years I never understood why, and it used to really bother me. But then one day I was driving my little boy to school, and I saw this quote by Walt Whitman, that was on the wall and it said, 'Be curious, not judgmental.'"

At that moment, Ted throws the first dart for a triple twenty and you can feel the energy in the room increase. He then states that as he gets back in his car and is driving, it hits him. "All of those fellas that used to belittle me, not a single one of them was curious. You know, they thought they had everything all figured out, so they judged everything and judged everyone. And then I realized they were underestimating me—who I was had nothing to do with it because if they were curious, they would have asked questions. Questions like, 'Have you played a lot of darts, Ted?'"

And just like that, another triple 20, and the crowd becomes boisterous and grows more excited as the anticipation builds down to the last dart. Then Ted states, "To which I would have answered, 'Yes, sir, every Sunday afternoon at a sports bar with my father from age 10 'til I was 16 until he passed away……barbecue sauce!" And boom, a game-ending bullseye, and the crowd erupts.

How many times have we judged a student, parent, or staff member without knowing anything about them? What if we would have just been a little bit more curious, and asked a few more questions? Core Principle 1 of *Culturize* reminds us that everyone has a story; therefore, we must be more intentional in our actions to understand those stories. When we fail to take the time to listen and dismiss the experiences of others, we can find ourselves placing a label on those same individuals we signed up to help.

The next time a "difficult" parent walks into the office upset, quickly reframe it and see them not as a difficult parent, but as a parent going through a difficult time. Although the difference in words may be subtle, they can impact our attitude and, ultimately, our response. A parent who is feeling the stress of losing a job, falling behind on their rent, struggling with their health, or carrying the burden of a broken relationship, needs our kindness and compassion. When we label others, whether it be adults or students, we hold them hostage by placing limits on them, eventually reducing their chances of having positive experiences or worse yet, reaching their full potential.

The 4 Most Powerful Words in Leadership

We have all encountered a student or staff member who ignored a request, pushed back on our comments, or even resisted our advice or support. We must be careful not to ignore these individuals. It's easy to ignore the resistors. Pay close attention to what they have to say. Everyone's voice and perspective matters.

Perhaps they see something through their lens that we don't see. What if we were to see it through their eyes? What would we see? Would we see it differently? I often recommend to those who work in schools, whether teachers working with students in the classroom, principals working with teachers and support staff, or superintendents working with school-based leaders, that it is important to come together as an entire team at least twice a year and recalibrate—to start over from a fresh point of reference to bring a newfound sense of hope and positively impact morale. We have all felt the grind of a school year and we know that a simple reboot can get us back on track and help everyone become more productive.

In this chapter, I will offer suggestions and provide different ways to recalibrate our people so they remain positively confident, but humble, in their work. To begin, let's take a look at the framework below to help you get back on track when you begin to feel the morale waiver a bit.

CULTURIZE VISION

BRING A GROUP OF PEOPLE TOGETHER

SHARE A VISION

4 MOST POWERFUL WORDS

UTILIZE A PROCESS

GIVE EVERYONE A VOICE

CREATE A PLAN

TAKE ACTION

1. **Bring a Group of People Together:** This can be a faculty meeting, a student assembly (classroom), a district principals' meeting, or a parent advisory meeting.
2. **Share a Vision:** What is it that you hope you accomplish? Be clear in your words.
3. **4 Most Powerful Words:** Leadership was never meant to be a committee of one, so use these words to inspire your team: I Need Your Help."
4. **Utilize a Process:** Be intentional in placing people on teams in which they are given both individual time and collaborative time to process responses.
5. **Give Everyone a Voice:** Allow people to reflect, share their reflections, and discuss their reflections.
6. **Create a Plan:** Give your team the time needed to plan effectively.
7. **Take Action:** Don't just be a planner. Be a doer, too.

When we are intentional in our actions, good things usually happen. Planning together is a great start, but working together leads to a great outcome.

Managing Student Discipline

Ask any teacher what they believe to be one of the biggest classroom challenges facing them in their work today with students and chances are they will bring up managing student behavior. Ask any administrator and you are likely to get the same response. I recall receiving an email from a teacher who was disgruntled with what she described as a lack of support from the administration regarding issues of student discipline. In her words, "Students are not being held accountable for their behavior and are allowed to do whatever they want because they know there won't be any consequences." I certainly understood her frustration. After all, it's not the first time I've heard such concerns raised. Not surprisingly, I've been privy to similar conversations with administrators regarding their frustrations with staff members who they felt either ignored inappropriate student behavior or in their words, "Just want the students punished."

So, this teacher's email got me thinking: Where is the disconnect? How can we begin to reflect on our practices to cultivate a school climate/culture in which both teachers and administration work together to carry the banner for one another in a positive way when it comes to addressing student behavior and acknowledging it is a challenging part of our work?

Consistency and clarity from the administrative team are critical here. The people we serve and lead must have a clear understanding of our expectations of them and for ourselves regarding student discipline. If teachers perceive a lack of clarity exists about how student behavior issues are expected to be handled, this is sure to cause consternation among both teachers and administration, not to mention the potential for students and families as well.

Here are five suggestions for administrators to begin addressing some of the common issues that are often shared with me when I am working with schools conducting cultural assessments:

a. **Avoid labeling students:** As adults, when we make mistakes or bad decisions, we often want others to withhold judgment, forgive us, give us a second or third chance, and not label us. Kids want and need the same thing from us. The student we label as a problem needs us during their most elevated moment. Reframe your thoughts so you don't see them as a difficult student, but rather a student going through a difficult time.

b. **Develop clear, well-defined expectations and procedures for student discipline:** This includes progressive, restorative discipline steps and the role of staff and administration in addressing student behaviors. It is best if these can be created by both administration and the entire staff (or building leadership team) together. Consider utilizing a 1-2-4 framework.

c. **Avoid delayed consequences:** The administrative team must work together to ensure that student referrals are addressed promptly. This needs to be consistent among all members of the administrative team. When a staff member issues a behavioral referral and does not receive communication back from the administration before the student returns to class, this can create resentment among even your strongest teachers.

d. **Circle back with student concerns:** This is a must-do if we want to gain support from those we lead. Most people understand matters of confidentiality, but it's also appropriate to share as much information as possible without violating confidentiality so teachers can empathize and support the administration. The more they know, the more they typically are willing to bend a little. They don't need to know all the details, but having some general information can be beneficial and sends a strong message that it takes a team approach to work with our most challenging students.

e. **Everyone is responsible for all students:** We can recognize the challenges that come with trying to discipline students we don't know well or who teachers have never had in class. In schools with strong cultures, there should be no such thing as "my kids" or "those kids." They are all "our kids." We should expect everyone to see all students as their students. In doing so, they don't need to intervene in every negative student behavior. We can recognize the challenges that come with trying to address behaviors with students we have never had in class, but at the very least, there needs to be an expectation to acknowledge inappropriate behavior and language when anyone encounters it. This begins to set the tone that certain behaviors are not acceptable and that everyone working at the school agrees with what is appropriate and what is not.

The way we communicate concerns or expectations can create negative undercurrents in the culture of schools. Teachers often express concerns about the way information is communicated by the administration, causing them to feel as though they are not doing enough and need to do more. This is often elevated by referral systems that are managed electronically. Whether this happens or not, if it is the perception among some staff members, it is enough to create issues among more people if they express this feeling privately to their colleagues. To minimize miscommunication, consider managing all conversations regarding student discipline face-to-face for some time. This would require the administration to walk students back to class or connect with staff members during a non-instructional time to discuss the resolution of the referral. By having the conversation face-to-face with students present, students will see staff and administration working together and this also reduces chances of miscommunication regarding expectations moving forward. When we recalibrate, trade time, and bring all parties together, we begin to create a process that leads to a higher standard regarding how we manage student discipline and build healthier relationships among students, staff, and administration.

Ditch Those Anonymous Surveys

Can I confess something to you? I always struggled to talk about work when I got home. Sometimes it was because I was just tired of talking. When things weren't going well, I had assistant principals to whom I could vent. You know the saying, "Misery loves company"? After unleashing my frustrations on them, I didn't feel like repeating myself all over again at home. Other times it was because I had to maintain the confidence of others who had shared things with me privately but added to the list of stresses I was already experiencing. And if I am being truthful, sometimes I was too upset, embarrassed, and ashamed because I didn't want to let down those who believed in me. The job of an educator can be a lonely world, and as my brother David (a professional magician) often reminds me, so can the life of a magician. I guess many can relate.

One night I took home the stress from a long day of feeling beat up. I remember being quiet, agitated, and in no mood to talk. It didn't take long for me to take the frustrations of the day out on my family. Sometimes those who love us the most are most vulnerable to experiencing the worst within us. I guess it is because we believe family is a safe place and, as educators, sometimes we need a safe place after another day of absorbing the emotions and the trauma of our students and colleagues. I remember saying, "You don't know what I have to deal with regularly. It doesn't matter how many hours I work, how many times I try to do the right thing, how many complaints I listen to, or how many times I go out of my way to help students, staff, and families, it will never be enough."

Earlier that night I had sat alone in my office, staring at the computer screen, full of anxiety, not wanting to click on the attachment. I knew what was about to come at me, and yet, I was going to have to take it (and carry it home with me), regardless if it was tainted with exaggerations, half-truths, or in some instances, flat-out lies. And with one click of the finger, I opened up a document that to this day, continues to wreak havoc on the psyche of educators everywhere and what I now consider the biggest culture killer of all—the Anonymous Survey.

How many times have you perused this anonymous list only to find yourself ignoring the positive comments handed out to you and focusing instead on the zingers being hurled at you? More importantly, why do we continue to use a tool that perpetuates the notion of mistrust that we are trying our darndest to combat, especially when we know that the foundation of every healthy culture is rooted in trust?

Truth be told, it is rare for me to come across a district that isn't currently using this practice to seek input from others. When I inquire why they are engaging in a tool that promotes anonymity and secrecy, they almost always respond, "Because if we don't, people won't tell us what they think; they won't be honest." When I press further to understand why someone wouldn't be truthful the follow up is often, "Because they worry if they are, they will get in trouble; there will be some sort of retaliation or retribution."

My response is typically the same: "So are you telling me that the only reason we are still using an anonymous survey is that if we don't, people won't tell us what they really think and the reason for that is because they worry they will get in trouble? If that is true, then what does that tell us about our culture?"

It is easy to create mission statements, post signs around campus, and pass out school profiles that promote excellence, but can a culture truly be considered excellent if we still must gather input anonymously? I think we have to ask ourselves this very tough question. I am not suggesting that schools blow up their entire systems. I am suggesting that at the very least, we counter this practice, which in my experience is ineffective, and balance it with a practice that has not only produced better results in our work but aligns with the premise of this chapter.

Eyes on Culture 1 on 1

Visionary leaders are often clear about the direction they want to go, but it's the humble leader who recognizes that she/he must listen to others to help them redirect that vision. What if you could recalibrate your culture with a more transparent survey that would counter or eliminate the anonymous survey and allow us to *See the Culture Through the Eyes of Others?* Face-to-face, 1:1 conversations could be implemented at all three levels. Superintendents could see culture through the eyes of principals, principals would use staff member input to see it, and teachers would ask students for their help. This, of course, would require an effective process to ensure a better result. Here are a few things to consider if you decide to move in this direction as a system and incorporate the *Eyes on Culture Survey* with staff and students:

> Visionary leaders are often clear about the direction they want to go, but it's the humble leader who recognizes that she/he must listen to others to help them redirect that vision.

1. **Purpose:** Introduce the *Eyes on Culture Survey* to explain the purpose of the survey. For example: We want to create a culture in which students and staff members can express their thoughts openly, without fear of repercussions.

2. **Transparency:** Questions should be provided in advance to give people time to process questions and prepare responses.

3. **Expectations:** Everyone will be expected to participate in interviews, but are not required to respond.
4. **Documentation:** All responses will be documented in writing and shared with the entire staff.
5. **Collaboration:** Everyone will review interview responses and help determine next steps to be taken.
6. **Agreements:** Once everyone comes to a consensus (Fist to Five) on actionable items, the implementation process will be monitored and measured.
7. **Communication:** The superintendent, principals, and teachers will maintain ongoing communication regarding the progress being made.
8. **Celebration:** Everyone comes together twice a year to celebrate positive changes resulting from the *Eyes on Culture Interview Survey*.

One word of caution for school and district leaders if you choose to move in this direction. If you ask for input, you must be willing to accept the responses. You cannot ask for feedback and then dismiss it or complain about it because it makes you uncomfortable or is considered controversial by some. Feedback can be a powerful tool to bring about positive change. It can also have negative consequences if we fail to do anything with it.

Our experience following this recalibration process has resulted in overwhelmingly positive responses and better outcomes. Of course, any aspect can be adapted and adjusted to meet the specific needs of each school community. However, to ensure the best possible outcomes, we encourage you to follow the process described here and most importantly, to model the practice at all three levels to make the greatest, most positive systemic change.

Below you will find example questions that you can use with principals, staff, and students:

EYES ON CULTURE: PRINCIPAL QUESTIONS

What part of your job gives you the most joy?

What are the work stresses that are keeping you up at night?

When you think about professionally, where you want to be a year from now, where do you see yourself? Where do you see yourself five years from today? How can I help support these goals?

How is life outside of work? Are you able to maintain a Life-Fit of personal and professional time commitments? What challenges are you currently facing?

What are the things that are currently frustrating you at work?

If you were to take over my role as Superintendent, what is one change you would make and why?

What is one facility improvement you would like to see happen in your building?

What is one belief as a leader that you used to have that has changed over the years that today you think differently about it?

Name one practice that we currently do in this district that you believe we need to stop doing. Why do you believe this?

In what ways can I best support you?

EYES ON CULTURE: STAFF QUESTIONS

What is currently going well in your work that brings you joy and a great sense of pride?

How do you feel supported by the district? Specifically, in what ways have you felt supported by me?

Can you share an experience you had at another workplace that would impact our culture in a positive way if we were to replicate it here?

What is one issue that you believe needs to be addressed right away that you think would lead to a more positive and healthier culture?

If you could remove one task from your current role, what would you remove and why?

What do you need from administration in order for you personally to feel supported so you can bring your best-self to work every day?

Is there a staff member you would like to recognize and why? Would you mind if I shared this with them?

EYES ON CULTURE: STUDENT QUESTIONS

What do you like most about this class?

How is this class different than the last class you attended?

What is one thing about this class that you wish I would change?

What do you need from me so you look forward to coming to class every day?

Is there one thing that I don't know about you that you would like to share with me?

I hope this class is a place that I can...

When I lose confidence I begin to...

I tend to do better when I can work...

When I get angry I...

One thing we must learn to accept as educators is that there will always be outliers—the people who support you regardless of your mistakes, and those who will never support you no matter your contributions. Regardless, we must continue to lead with integrity.

Excuses or Exposure?

When I look back on my career as an educator, all sorts of thoughts and emotions run through my mind. I know I was not prepared for all the situations I would encounter both as a teacher and as a principal. The pressures I experienced, the failures I endured, and the criticisms that came my way; most have subsided, but mainly by choice. What remains intact since walking away from campus leadership to start my own company are the abundance of memories, blessings, and joyfulness I feel from the work I was able to do and the connections I was able to make. Those will forever be etched in my mind.

Every job I have had in my life brought with it long hours, a certain level of isolation and loneliness, a high level of commitment, and an immense amount of pressure to succeed. I don't believe anyone or any job is immune from that.

I wish I could fix all the problems that educators encounter, but I cannot. I often state during my presentations that I am not a magician. I leave that to my brother David, who I mentioned briefly in the last section. He is damn good at what he does. Yes, he can wow you and make things appear and disappear, but my sleight of hand is not up to his caliber. He has been practicing his craft since he was a sophomore in high school.

One day I was watching him with great pride as he was dazzling a crowd with card tricks. One such trick called for him to have a person select a card from the deck, sign it, and then place the card back into the deck. He let the person cut the deck, and shuffle the cards, all while he chatted with the crowd to keep them engaged. Once the deck of cards was handed back to him, he did a few quick fancy cuts and shuffles that were impressive on their own. And in a moment of great anticipation, he laid the deck down and asked the person to turn over the top card. The look and sound of disappointment quickly came from the crowd as the card he turned over was not his card.

David gave a look of confusion. Then, he reached into his pocket and pulled out a small card that was folded up in a paperclip, and slowly opened it up. Upon seeing the signed card, he handed it back to this person. The crowd erupted into loud cheers and applause.

My brother, forever the showman, stated, "Thank you. You just witnessed twenty years of my life in one minute. It's a lonely world, my friends."

Yes, it can be. Choose any profession and these same feelings that we all experience as educators will be no different for them. The grass isn't always greener somewhere else.

That is why I struggle today when I see my fellow educators going to public domains to share their frustrations about our profession. I don't begrudge them and I am not saying they shouldn't or that they are even wrong to do so. I am just expressing my concern about the long-term potential damage that could come from this. I am worried we actually may be turning people away from considering a career in education by dwelling too much on its negative aspects. If we desire our young people to consider teaching as a future career choice, then I believe we need to highlight the positive benefits of this noble profession. Turn on any television or pull up most social media platforms and you can get a sense of what is happening to our profession. According to a January 2022 survey of National Education Association members, more than 55% of teachers say they are likely to leave the profession sooner than planned because of the pandemic, almost double since the last report in 2020. And for principals, the news is not much better. The National Association of Secondary School Principals (NASSP) survey states that 40% of school leaders report the negative impact of the pandemic has accelerated their plan to leave the profession in the next three years (Ruggirello, Wallace Blog, 2022).

I am blessed that my daily travels take me all across the country and I can experience different schools with different people and different cultures and different communities. Ironically, however, the cultural issues of these schools remain relatively the same, regardless of the size, location, and demographic population of the school community—with low morale among teachers and support staff leading the way. Teachers are stressed and worried about their students, and rightfully so. The feeling among many teachers I talk to is that their students are unmotivated and behave in ways that make it difficult for them to teach. As for school and district leaders, they state that the fallout from the pandemic seems to be the number one reason for many of the issues and challenges they continue to encounter when it comes to teacher behavior and the perception of increased negativity among their staff regarding student performance—both academically and behaviorally. It would be hard for anyone to deny the negative impact the pandemic has had on our schools, including kids, educators, and families. Yes, the pandemic turned our world upside down, but at what point do we as a profession move forward with the business of school, and focus on teaching and learning again without using Covid-19 as a crutch? I give every member of our school communities all the accolades they deserve for their efforts, persistence, and unwavering commitment to their students. However, there is a potential danger that lies beneath the surface that I want to point out.

I am worried that the pandemic has become our "go-to" excuse for many of the problems we are currently facing. With your permission, I would like to pose this fundamental question: Is it possible that the pandemic is not the sole cause of many of our current issues, and, instead, it merely exposed matters that were already prevalent in many schools? If you are in the camp that a culture of excellence requires a healthy culture (defined earlier as a place where you look forward to going each day because you feel connected, valued, appreciated, and inspired and where you are given a voice to be a part of something bigger, something meaningful, and you believe that together with your peers, you can accomplish anything), then perhaps that healthy culture didn't exist before the pandemic came along and kicked us in the ass. And if that is the case, then even more reason why campuses everywhere should take time to recalibrate and ask themselves, "Is our current culture healthy enough to dig us out of this morale funk we currently find ourselves in?" A healthy culture looks at its current reality and envisions a new desired reality, and then comes together as a school community to reframe it, and change their results by changing their responses and their behaviors.

Avoiding Negative Undercurrents

In 2020, I wrote *Live Your Excellence* as an attempt to tackle the issues in schools not many want to think or talk about: the dangerous undercurrents that form when we're afraid to have difficult conversations. A conventional response to these dangerous undercurrents would be to make people *comply* with "the rules." Having worked hard to learn from my past mistakes, today I am committed to trying to better myself in every aspect of my life, including trying to help others navigate the same treacherous undercurrents of compliance I was once responsible for.

Rather than let ourselves get caught on the perimeter and get swept away in a riptide of mistakes, how can we avoid creating the undercurrents altogether? None of us has an owner's manual on how to do this, but there are things that we can do to reframe our thinking so we can relieve ourselves from the pressures of needing to have all the answers. The potential danger of renting this feeling is that you will pay for it in many ways—stress, burden, the weight of the world, and worry of failure.

In the last chapter, I shared the negative impact that can result when we don't look at our inner self when things don't turn out the way we want them to. I looked to blame Pam when the money came up missing. I was not able to recognize at that time that the moment I blamed her I created an undercurrent. In fact, I created more than one and I paid for it. The undercurrents were forming as soon as I delegated a task to her without a proper framework. I also failed to invest the necessary time to ensure that she knew exactly what I needed her to do and how I needed her to do it. I should have looked at my behavior; instead, I looked at the perimeter, focusing on her behavior.

As much as I did not want to see it at the time, Jim challenged me with the following question that would forever change the way I viewed myself as a leader: "Is this a teacher issue or a leadership issue?" I took a moment to reflect on his question and within seconds I had a revelation. Not only could I see that this was a leadership issue, but I also saw something else—I was the undercurrent.

Much of my work today involves me observing and coaching educators. I try to bring clarity to how we can all quickly fall victim to becoming the undercurrent: in our classrooms as teachers, our buildings as principals, and our campuses as district office administrators. Undercurrents can easily form when we delegate responsibilities to others, regardless of our role. When teachers attempt to empower students but do not use a clear framework for doing so, they increase the chances of not achieving the results they want and then run the risk of blaming the student. If you ever find yourself in this scenario and want to avoid the perimeter, reframe it and ask yourself, "Is this a student issue or teacher issue?" More than likely, you will learn that not always, but often, *we* are the undercurrent. This new way of thinking—inner leadership before perimeter leadership—will require an intentional effort on your part to pause and begin with an inner reflection to see what you could have done differently to attain a better result. The more you instill this type of thinking, the more you will see a better version of you evolve over time.

In the pages to follow, I will share a few common undercurrents that I observe in my daily work. I will also provide a reframing for you to consider so that you may see it through the eyes of others and avoid a negative undercurrent. I have described other common undercurrents previously, including ineffective meetings, lack of functional leadership teams, complex conversations, and anonymous surveys. Although I did not specifically identify them as such, as you look back, I hope that you can now see how these practices can create undercurrents and negatively impact your culture.

Committees

When we identify a few members to lead a committee, it can send an unintended message that those individuals are responsible for addressing an issue. If you have ever been on the receiving end of harsh criticism you know what I am sharing here has merit. Regardless of whether you were assigned or volunteered for committee work, when you spend any amount of time on additional tasks outside your teaching responsibilities and encounter criticism based on your suggestions or recommendations, it can create an undercurrent of resentment when we are not appreciated for our time and effort.

Committee work can be effective when we are clear in defining and communicating the roles and responsibilities of committee members to the entire staff. I would argue that committee work should include researching and gathering information, organizing and preparing the information or data, and facilitating or presenting the information to others. What it should not include is the committee making the final decisions about any changes to practices, protocols, or policies. For example, the attendance committee is not responsible for creating new guidelines for attendance. That is not their responsibility. That responsibility lies with the entire staff. Using the 1 -2 - 4 Framework, I believe that every one of us can have a voice and take responsibility for addressing the attendance issues that exist in our schools. Only by working together to learn the reasons behind those absences, can we begin to understand the required support that students, teachers, families, and administration will need to positively impact the overall student attendance data.

Favorites

One of the deepest undercurrents that both teachers and administrators create is the perception among others that we have our favorites. Students often share stories of favoritism displayed towards certain segments of the student population and teachers view some of their colleagues as having the ear of their administrators or receiving favorable perks because of their relationship with the administration.

To avoid this undercurrent will first require a shift in our thinking where we will want to begin to view every student and every teacher as our favorite. If we allow our biases to cloud our view of others or our experiences to jade the way we feel about some of our students or staff members, we will continue to draw criticisms of favoritism from those who feel ignored or underappreciated for their talents or efforts. Moreover, it will require a change in our approach when seeking opinions, input, or support from others. We must be intentional in using a process whereby everyone gets an opportunity to have a voice or is invited to participate in a specific task or event. One example would include asking certain individuals to present at a faculty meeting or asking students to stay after school to help with a class project. When we seek out some people and leave other people out of such opportunities, we can create an undercurrent of both jealousy and resentment. In addition, over the long term, we can encounter additional undercurrents from those individuals we regularly seek out. Even our best students and staff can eventually begin to keep score and tire of having to add more to their plates while their counterparts avoid these same added tasks.

Risk-Taking

How often throughout your career have you been told to think outside the box or been encouraged or even given permission to be creative or innovative? How many times have you expressed similar sentiments to your students? Perhaps never or perhaps more than you can recall. When students and educators hear these comments shared, it can create a sense of excitement and positive energy, especially among those who love to tap into their creative juices or enjoy the challenge of stretching the limits. Consequently, nothing deflates a culture of risk-taking faster than, when a new idea is shared, we immediately hesitate and begin to share a plethora of reasons why an idea might not be doable. These reasons can range from safety concerns to lack of funding, to managing logistics, to the hoop-jumping associated with seeking approval from higher-ups.

Minimizing these undercurrents will necessitate a reframing of our mindset and a recalibration of our actions that leave student and staff risk-takers walking away more excited about their ideas than they were before they presented them to us. If students and staff walk away dejected, we need to reassess our responses and move away from expressing our concerns to sharing our excitement if we aim to cultivate a culture of risk-taking. This does not mean that students and staff should never be told no. It means we need a more effective process whereby we spend more time being curious and asking questions, but asking them in a way that demonstrates a willingness on our part to figure out a way to make some of it, if not all of it, come to fruition.

Rather than kill dreams, let's make the dreams happen by providing the support, ideas, belief, guidance, resources, and time to help work through the challenges so others can see our willingness to be risk-takers as well.

Faculty Meetings

Teachers should create a positive learning experience in the classroom that makes students look forward to coming back the next day excited and ready to learn again. I have met hundreds of teachers over my career who were able to achieve this feeling with many of their students. During my time as principal, I did my best to express my gratitude to these teachers because not only did they impact students in a way that every child deserves to be impacted, they also made my job easier.

One afternoon I was meeting with a teacher and, unintentionally, made a comment that came across as a comparison to another teacher and her ability to create an environment for kids that was truly impactful. Although I did not see it at the time, my comparison devalued the work this teacher had done with her students, especially considering the special challenges many of them were facing. My comments had come across as insensitive and hurtful. Later that evening I received an email from this teacher who was able to articulate respectfully and professionally how my comments had made her feel. She was right and I felt terrible that I had hurt her in that way.

The next morning, I stopped by to apologize and during our conversation, she shared something with me that made me reflect. "I appreciate the level of expectations placed on us to create a classroom environment for our students that you described, but if you are going to place such an expectation on us, should you not hold yourself accountable to the same standard," she stated.

"I agree, but can you tell me what you mean?" I asked.

"Well, some of us were talking the other day and someone shared that our faculty meetings can be hard to sit through. A couple of others expressed the same sentiment and, speaking for myself, I kind of have to agree. I hope you know that I only share this with you because we do enjoy seeing each other, but it would be even better if we got more out of them. When you were talking to me yesterday, that is what was going through my mind—that we deserve to walk away looking forward to wanting to come back just like our students."

There was nothing I could do at the moment other than thank her for sharing how she felt. She was right.

As principals, every time we bring our staff together, it is like teaching a class and our staff members are our students. The same can be said of superintendents when holding principal meetings. Our teachers deserve to look forward to attending faculty meetings, no differently than students should be excited about attending class. And like our students, teachers know what makes them want to come back the next day ready to learn. All we need to do is ask them for their help in managing our faculty meetings in the same way, an effective teacher plans and teaches a meaningful lesson in their classroom—Core Principle 2. When our classroom, building, and district office practices begin to mirror each other, we establish a healthier learning environment for all students and staff and reduce the number of ever-exhausting undercurrents.

Onboarding New Staff

Last November, I visited a school and the principal asked if I could meet with her instructional coach. Sam was in her first year as an instructional coach and was struggling to adapt to her new role. She elaborated on a few concerns she was having with a few teachers. She shared that some teachers seemed non-receptive to her being in their classrooms. Others were open to the idea but weren't sure what her role was or how she could support them. Sam shared that she felt overwhelmed and was having trouble efficiently scheduling her work so that she could help more teachers. Four months into her new role and she was questioning herself. She went so far as to share with me privately that she wondered if she had made a mistake taking on this new position.

As educators, we all know the challenges of starting a new position and the nervous feelings that we experience when we first step into our new role. We can become consumed with all the worries, whether we are first-year beginning teachers or seasoned veterans. The way we transition new employees can make the difference between a great experience and a poor experience. If we aim to set up our new staff members and staff members moving into new roles for success, we must be intentional in providing opportunities for connections to ensure that they feel a sense of belonging—like they are a part of their new team from the get-go. Coincidentally, teachers must see how this relates to them when new students join their class after the start of a school year. When teachers are intentional in building personal relationships and connecting new students to their peers during their transition, it can mitigate a student's level of anxiety and elevate them to new heights of belonging.

Beyond connection, all team members must understand the role, responsibilities, and expectations they each will have to ensure the transition will reap the greatest benefit. Ultimately, this will inspire each team member to carry the banner for one another because of the incredible experience they had. When it comes to the success of any high-performing culture, I believe that we all play a major role. Although no one person should have to carry that burden, effective teachers and leaders are intentional in communicating expectations. Expectations should never be left to chance.

Let's revisit Sam's experience above. As I have shared previously, a poor process will garner a poor result. As Sam described her experience to me, it was clear that the principal had missed an opportunity to effectively onboard Sam into her new role as an Instructional Coach. Please note that by all accounts this principal was an effective leader. She was an experienced principal who had worked in the school for several years. The school had received several awards for excellence during her tenure and she was well-respected by students and staff alike. Yet, here she was feeling like a failure because she believed that she had let Sam down. It is a reminder for all of us, that regardless of how long we serve in this profession, there will be days when we fall short of our expectations. We are, after all, human. What matters is that we recognize our deficiencies, acknowledge when we fall short, and work with our team to identify, design, and implement a better process to support our people so they may have a better experience. In this case, the principal did not disappoint. Working with Sam, we revisited the transition into her new role and developed a clear process to support her moving forward. Examine the following steps below:

Administrative Steps to On-Board Instructional Coaches (IC)
Note: *This is specific to Instructional Coaches due to their unique position.*

1. Share your overall vision of building a community of leaders and learners.
   - Cultivate a culture where everyone sees themselves as an IC. One person serving in this role is a good start, but greatness comes from building a system of support that is sustainable.
2. Gather feedback on classroom needs from all staff.
   - Identify specific areas that IC's will focus on when working with staff. Limit to no more than three (3) items that can be measured so data can be collected and results shared out.
3. Identify the specific role and responsibility of IC.
   - In addition to the three areas identified above, in what other ways will IC's serve staff? Define what is appropriate (collect data, lesson design, classroom management, modeling, co-teaching, etc.) and not appropriate (grading, data input, running errands, making copies, ordering supplies, contacting parents, managing Individualized Education Plans, etc.)

4. Be clear in your expectations of staff in welcoming IC into all classrooms.
    *   IC's will work with all teachers and teachers will be open to supporting the work of ICs and partner with them to meet the overall building goals.
5. Work with the building leadership team to identify individual needs.
    *   Empower BLT to develop processes and tools to identify and provide equitable support to individuals while also focusing on building-wide goals.
6. Determine data points to be collected and shared out.
    *   Work with BLT on specific data to be collected and shared with all staff weekly.
7. Describe the purpose of weekly meetings with IC.
    *   Schedule weekly meetings to support IC and overall vision. The purpose is to communicate overall progress, challenges, and successes, to ensure the overall success of IC and the quality of service provided to all staff.
8. Maintain integrity, trust, and confidentiality of IC and teacher support.
    *   Conversations should not identify specific staff members. Confidentiality is critical. Discussions should be global.
9. Create a plan to multiply the community of IC's.
    *   Work with BLT to create a plan for all teachers to visit and support peers in specific areas agreed to by the team. Start with BLT members and build from there.
10. Monitor progress and communicate results to all staff. Celebrate successes.
    *   Maintain weekly communications on progress. Transparency is key. Be sure to highlight and celebrate ongoing successes monthly.

Regardless of the level–classroom, building, or district office–each community must expect excellence and support one another in clearly identifying, modeling, and replicating processes to ensure equitable practices for all stakeholders across the system. Sam did not have a good experience as she transitioned into her new role as an IC. She was drowning and was looking to return to her previous position as a 5th-grade teacher where she had a positive, successful experience for several years. We often see these undercurrents develop with teachers and administrators as they move into their new roles. Below, you will find a framework to consider for helping minimize the depth of potential undercurrents as you transition new employees into your district. The steps are intended to align with the core principles of *Culturize*: Principle #1 - Be a champion by investing time in others (relationships) and Principle #3 - Create an experience so others will carry the banner for you because of the way you made them feel.

Administrative Steps to On-Board New Staff

1. Re-Connection Call
   • The administration calls candidates after they have been offered a position to stay in contact and communication throughout the summer months. If we believe that the foundation of excellent cultures is rooted in relationships, then we must go beyond saying it and show it by investing time in others. There are many other benefits to doing this, but most importantly it models your willingness to live the core principles.

2. 1:1 Meetings
   • Once new hires arrive on campus, schedule monthly meetings individually to stay connected. Maintaining a pulse on the morale of new staff is a critical component of the onboarding process.

3. Monthly Cohort Meetings
   • Individual meetings are powerful because of the personal connections that you make, but you also want to cultivate those relationships among all of your new hires. Monthly meetings as a cohort will allow for interconnections among grade levels and departments as well as connect teachers to non-certified staff.

4. Monthly Workshops
   • Use these before or after-school workshops as an opportunity to invest in your new staff and re-invest in your veteran staff. Invite veteran staff members to do training on different topics that support beginning teachers and support staff.

5. Coaching Observations
   • Be intentional in scheduling ongoing coaching observations through the first year to support staff and ensure their growth so they maintain their passion and desire to be the best they can be for others and themselves.

The onboarding of new staff must be a priority. This begins by incorporating the values of connectivity and meaningful experiences during the transition period. When we are intentional with our time and follow a framework for transitioning new employees, we reduce the potential for undercurrents to develop.

Non-Renewal of Staff

The end of a school year can bring about a host of challenges for building and district leaders. Included in those challenges are those that can take an emotional toll on even the strongest of leaders. Every so often, an administrator is faced with the decision of whether to renew or non-renew an employee's contract. These moments are difficult and stressful for both the employee and the administrator who is responsible for making the final decision because, in some regards, we are potentially taking away a person's livelihood. No matter how it is presented, it is difficult for anyone not to take this conversation personally and blame the messenger when they are told they will not be returning the following year. The undercurrent that is generated from this conversation is often made stronger in two ways—the way the message is communicated and the timing of the communication. As leaders, we have control over both of these variables.

Let's assume for a moment that you have an employee whose performance is not living up to your expectations or standards. For this example, we will remove conduct that is unbecoming of an educator that would get them immediately suspended or terminated due to the severity of the violation. Instead, we will focus on a teacher who demonstrates a deficiency in instructional practices, student engagement, classroom management, poor academic results, or abuse of attendance policies. In other words, we are dealing with an underperforming employee, the most common reason for the non-renewal of employees.

If an employee is notified of this news at the time the final summative evaluations are due, the potential for this to come across as a "gotcha" quickly increases. No one wants to be caught off guard, especially when it involves the status of your employment. Have you ever experienced or known of someone who has been involved in a similar situation where this type of news was delivered and the response was argumentative or one of anger, denial, or emotional crying? Did the news result in a long rebuttal letter, complaint, additional meetings, grievance, or the worst-case scenario, litigation? If so, be careful not to move out to the perimeter too quickly. Let me explain.

When an employee is categorized as underperforming, it is likely that this is not an issue that arose in recent weeks. Most often, they have been struggling for months and in some cases, years. To mitigate the potential for an undercurrent, or at a minimum reduce the depth of the undercurrent in this scenario, the fair thing would have been to notify the employee of your intentions to non-renew much earlier in the process. In other words, when it comes to underperformance, we should never include concerns, especially an issue of intent to non-renew an employee, without them not being fully aware of the situation. Typically, I recommend those conversations take place as soon as it becomes a strong possibility, certainly no later than mid-year to allow them to seek employment elsewhere and within a period (early spring) when they can pursue other job interviews.

Nevertheless, you could manage the conversation effectively and communicate your intent early on and still end up with the same result. However, we also know that when we reflect on our behaviors and self-assess our practices, we will more often than not produce a better result because of the way we manage a particular situation.

Not Everything Is a Level 10

As I approached the main entrance, I could see that Larry was agitated about something based on his body language and facial expressions. "What's going on?" I asked.

"It's been crazy around here," he responded.

"Tell me more," I said.

As we walked to his office Larry began to describe a plethora of incidents that had occurred the day before. As we entered his office I responded, "Sounds like you had one of those days, my friend."

"Yes, indeed", Larry stated. "It was absolutely nuts and I am still irritated."

Larry continued with one story after another for the next twenty minutes. It was clear that he needed to vent about his day, so I let him because I felt that is what he needed from me at that moment.

"Can I ask you to do me a favor Larry," I asked.

"Sure, what?" said Larry.

"Take this sticky note and write down the five things that upset you the most yesterday." Larry gave me a puzzled look and then began to write. When he finished I said, "Now give each item a ranking between 1 and 10, with 10 representing your highest stress point, your greatest frustration."

When Larry finished he handed me back the sticky note listing of few of the incidents from the previous day with the following rankings:

Students vaping in the bathroom - 10

Student pulled the fire alarm - 10

Students throwing baby carrots at lunch - 9

Teacher called in sick for the third day in a row and the sub didn't have any lesson plans. Sub sent nine students to the office - 9

Teacher complained that another teacher was disrespectful in their team meeting and is requesting a transfer to a new team - 8

"I can keep going if you want me to," exclaimed Larry.

I smiled, "That won't be necessary, buddy. Will you permit me to help you try and reframe this?" I asked.

"Sure, but I am not convinced it will do much good," he responded.

I looked at Larry and raising my left hand to eye level I said, "10 - Intruder in the building posing a threat to others. 10 - Student or staff medical emergency. Anything that pertains to the safety of your students or staff, depending on the level of danger should be rated in the 8 to 10 range, including weapons, use/selling of illegal substances, and physical assault. Ratings of 5 to 7 would include any severe policy violations, such as inappropriate use of technology, bullying, verbal abuse, low-level threats, vandalism, theft, etc. A rating of 3-4 could include profanity, insubordination, minor disrespect, and finally, a rating of 1-2, students are refusing to work, skipping class, not sitting in assigned seats, dress-code violation, rude behavior, and so on. Not everything is an eight, nine, or ten, but I am worried that is what you are ranking these incidents. And if you rank them at that level, your staff will, too. If we are not careful, our teachers will absorb our level of intensity and I don't want you renting or leasing out that feeling."

LEVEL	EXAMPLES
8-10	**PERTAINS TO THE SAFETY OF STUDENTS/STAFF** (intruder, medical emergency, physical assault, illegal substances, etc.)
5-7	**SEVERE POLICY VIOLATIONS** (bullying, inappropriate technology use, vandalism, theft, etc.)
3-4	**POLICY VIOLATIONS** (insubordination, profanity, minor disrespect etc.)
1-2	**MINOR POLICY VIOLATIONS** (dress-code, work refusal, rude behavior, etc.)

Larry and I continued our discussion, going and back forth to what constituted a two, five, seven, etc. What I appreciated most about Larry was that he understood this activity was designed to get him to look at things differently, reframing the incidents in his school to avoid overreacting, getting over-emotional, or elevating all things to a ten. I reminded him that this would not resolve his frustrations, but if he were to think about things differently, it would influence his response and produce better overall results.

Larry thanked me for the conversation and stuck his sticky note on his computer and then quickly moved on to the next thing. He then reached into his desk drawer and pulled out a box.

"What do you think?" he asked.

"What are they?" I responded.

"They are magnetic name tags. I purchased one for every student to help us all learn their names. I was wondering if you would like to help me pass them out this afternoon," Larry asked.

"Sure, I would love to," I responded.

Two days later I received a text message from Larry asking me to give him a call. "What's up?" I asked.

"I have to tell you about something that happened this morning," Larry replied. "I was in my office when my secretary called me and told me I was needed in the 7th-grade hallway right away. I hurried over there and when I came around the corner, three of my teachers were standing there and I could tell they were upset about something based on their body language and the way they were pointing. As I approached them I could hear one of the teachers complaining about how our kids don't respect anything and so on. She pointed up and stuck to the ceiling were over a dozen name tags. I couldn't believe it. I was so mad I called my secretary and told her to get a custodian with a ladder over here ASAP and take down the name tags to find out who the culprits were. I thanked the teachers and told them I would be contacting their parents and sending them all home once I returned to my office. I'm telling you, Jimmy, I was upset. I sat down and took out my notepad and then I looked at my computer and there was the post-it note. I looked at it closer and thought to myself, 'Crap, this is a one.'"

I am not suggesting that students should not be disciplined for inappropriate behaviors or that people should not receive consequences when they breach a policy. What I am suggesting is to keep things in perspective and respond accordingly based on a comparison of how serious one violation is compared to another. Larry saw it at that moment. He quickly reframed it and rather than suspend this group of students and potentially create undercurrents with the families of these students, he used it as an opportunity to build relationships with his kids. He met with them all together to hear their side of the story and when he inquired why they had done this, one student told him he was tossing his name tag in the air when it accidentally stuck to the ceiling. He had no idea the ceiling was metal. He told his friends about it and of course, they wanted to see if theirs would stick too. Why? Because that is what 7th graders sometimes do!

Can you Identify one event in hindsight when you may have caused an undercurrent that resulted in you hurting your culture (trust, hurt feelings, perception of you, etc.) Now ask yourself, what is within your capacity to mediate the undercurrents? Our egos can make us stubborn at times. Most of us don't want to begin by looking internally to see how we contribute to the undercurrents. This is another reason why we must take time to recalibrate as a staff. A perspective of shared ownership will not only help us see it differently but help us to respond differently to it as well. Undercurrents are like smoke in your eyes. They will burn you if you aren't paying attention. So I started paying attention. It took me years to see that more often than not, *I* was the undercurrent. Your challenge will come in the unlearning, as it did for me. What are you willing to unlearn? Are you willing to let things go that in most cases, have been staples in your practice for years and yet, have contributed to your undercurrents? This will take both courage and intentional discipline on your part. Lip service will not work. To cultivate hope you

> If you pay attention, you will find the undercurrents are talking to you and you need to listen to them.

will need to first pay attention. If you pay attention, you will find the undercurrents are talking to you and you need to listen to them. The more you listen, the more you will avoid them, and, over time, you will see them more clearly and continue to grow and develop into a better version of yourself.

References:

Why You Laughing?, 2020, September 19. Ted Lasso. Dart Game [Video]. YouTube. https://www.youtube.com/watch?v=oZ4YSXv6X kg&ab_channel=WhyYouLaughing%3F

Ruggirello, Andrea. *New Research Points to a Looming Principal Shortage.* Wallace Blog, February 23, 2022.

Reflect AND
RECALIBRATE

(Use the following space for reflective notes)

CHAPTER 5

Premise 4: Average Exists in Every Organization

The best days are often the ones we approach like
we've decided to go for it.

I n the last two years, I've spoken to dozens of educators who have shared with me privately they are planning on leaving their current position. Only a couple mentioned their safety as the primary reason for them contemplating leaving. A few of them talked about how they didn't feel valued and appreciated while some indicated they no longer felt challenged. Some said they were just ready for a change, exhausted by the events of the last two years. But it was the ones who mentioned how unhappy they were that saddened me the most.

Personally, it is hard for me to see good people who are struggling. Xavier was one of those teachers who reached out to me for advice. He shared with me how over the top excited he was about moving to his new school. He was grateful for the time he had spent teaching at his last school, having started there straight out of college. However, to return to his alma mater to teach and coach was a once-in-a-lifetime opportunity that he couldn't pass up. He described how during the interview process he had learned that the school had been designated as a failing school, but that he wasn't concerned. He saw this as an opportunity to be part of rebuilding a program that he, along with his colleagues and the community, could be proud of. He admitted he had underestimated how bad things were. The principal that hired him had been replaced midway through his second year and he, along with many of his colleagues, was having difficulty adapting to the new principal's leadership style, which he described as intimidating. In the four years since Xavier had started working there, thirty members of the staff of sixty had turned over.

I continue to encounter similar stories to the one described above. Teachers, support staff, and administrators all find themselves working in cultures in which they are merely trying to survive, similar to a fight, flight, or flee response. This was the case for Xavier. He openly admitted that he was in survival mode, most days knowing he was no longer giving it his all. Xavier stated he feared for his job, which some days left him feeling stuck, almost paralyzed, worried that at any moment, he would be summoned to the office. This is a common response in environments where people are constantly afraid. Days when he thought the administration was going to retaliate for challenging some of the current thinking were the most stressful. The chaos left him guarded and ready to fight, but also wore him out. The constant worry and fear left him somewhat traumatized. It is this type of trauma that creates the conditions for average to become the standard in the school environment, and in some cases, permeate throughout the entire system. This systemic trauma can look different across classrooms, buildings, and entire campuses because of the differences in people's natural responses to serving in an environment in which they do not feel safe.

Xavier's story left an empty feeling in my gut. Four years ago, he was looking forward to returning to the school where he once excelled as a student both in the classroom and the field. Now he was seeking my advice as he contemplated a career change.

Is It Time for a Change?

When I am asked this question by educators I cross paths with in my travels, I respond in the same manner that I would respond to those who I support today in my work as a leadership coach. A few of the questions I pose for them to reflect upon include the following:

1. When you think about leaving, what are the reasons that come to mind?
2. Do you ever think about the reason(s) why you feel the way you feel and what is causing it?
3. How does your family feel about the prospect of you leaving?
4. What risks do you think there would be by seeking a new position?
5. What type of work makes you the happiest?
6. Are there any internal candidates for the new position you are seeking?
7. How do you think you would respond if you didn't get the position?
8. What do you think your new team would bring to you that your current team doesn't provide?
9. How do you feel each day when you walk into work?
10. Have you accomplished everything you set out to do? If not, why not?
11. Are you ready to face the type of scrutiny and gossip that sometimes comes with leaving your current job for a new position?
12. Are you ready to commit the time it will take to make the type of impact your new school community deserves?

I often think about this quote from Steve Jobs. "Your work is going to fill a large part of your life, and the only way to be truly satisfied is to do what you believe is great work. And the only way to do great work is to love what you do." (Steve Jobs, Commencement Speech, 2005)

If you are considering leaving your current job, school or district, take time to reflect on these comments, questions, and responses I have shared with others over the years. I don't profess to think that doing so will bring perfect clarity to your situation, but hopefully, it will cause you to pause and reflect in a manner that brings you peace of mind and helps you avoid the pitfalls I have seen others I care about experience from time and time.

Top 8 Rules of Work Engagement:

+ We should never begin "looking" until we have given our supervisor, principal, or superintendent the respect and courtesy she/he deserves by letting her/him know. In my opinion, not doing so reflects poorly on our character and could cause others to question our integrity and lead to issues of mistrust should they hear from someone else that you are looking to leave.

+ If we are unhappy with our current situation, we should ask ourselves if we have communicated to our supervisor how we feel. By doing so we also allow her/him the opportunity to "fix it." It's not ours to judge whether we think it will do any good. The responsibility is ours to provide the same opportunity that we would want others to give us—a chance to address someone's concern.

+ There will come a time when we recognize that someone we work with or for does not have a skill set equal to our own. The question we should ask ourselves is what are we doing to help her/him get better. Great leaders help others around them elevate their performance and, in many cases, they allow others around them to help them get better as well.

+ Not every boss, principal, superintendent, etc. is going to let us do all the things we would like to do. I often will hear others tell me their supervisor won't let them do what they want or feel they need to do. My response? You can choose to do nothing, thereby guaranteeing the status quo remains in place or you can do everything in your power to surround yourself with others who share the same passion and work together to influence change positively regardless of the skill set of the leader. Either way, it's a choice.

+ Don't take a new position if you know it's not the right time. Let me say this. I have seen many "once in a lifetime opportunities" come around again. Stay patient and weigh all the benefits and disadvantages of such a move. Never accept a job at the moment it is offered that is based solely on emotion.

+ If what is holding you back is you are afraid you will miss your students, guess what? You will! However, you will quickly learn that kids everywhere, regardless of race, gender, or socioeconomic class, need positive adults in their lives to support, encourage, challenge, inspire, and love them. In a child's world, their issues are real regardless of what we believe to be the level of importance in our minds.

+ Be careful what you wish for. For those who have never worked in another school or district, it can be easy to perceive that things will be so much better somewhere else. This calls for a period of reflection, but maybe not in the way you think I am suggesting. What I mean is that we should always reflect on our attitudes and behaviors and try to determine what role we play in our dissatisfaction with our current situation.

+ Always reach out to others to help you gain a broader perspective in terms of motivation and fears. In my opinion, we all have them. It's okay to admit you do.

Sometimes professionally it feels right, but personally, something seems amiss, and at other times, the reverse is true. If a new challenge is what you desire, I would argue that for some of us, those challenges already exist in our current roles. A colleague once shared with me that our working lives should be more like running a marathon than a sprint. Not only do I agree with him, but what I have also learned over the years is that success is in the journey regardless of where it takes us. If you are wondering, "Is it time for a change?" and "What will happen if it doesn't work out?" I would argue that there is no risk for those who have a high skill set because if things don't turn out the way you had hoped, you will still have other options because of that skill set. If you are contemplating leaving but worry that it may not be the perfect fit, remember that some people turn their new environment into a perfect fit because the best people know how to "fit in" no matter where they go.

Is it time for a change? It is if it no longer feels right or you are not happy. Trust me. You will know it when the time comes. Either way, it's our choice in how we navigate our current circumstances that ultimately will determine how our journey ends or, for that matter, begins anew. Just be sure to let your supervisor know how you are feeling. They deserve to hear it from you first.

This Is Going to Hurt

I still catch myself flinching now and then while driving. My triggers are consistent for the most part. I can get a little jumpy when I approach an intersection and a vehicle begins to slowly crawl out. I find myself looking back and forth over and over before pulling out into a busy intersection. The sight of a car parked on the side of a highway or interstate triggers the most fear in me. If you don't know anything about my life's experiences you might think I am an overly cautious defensive driver. I wasn't always, but today I certainly am.

I knew I was in trouble. At the last second, I was able to swerve just enough to avoid a direct head-on collision. I can only imagine how much worse the outcome would have been having not done so. In the days and weeks following the accident, people would ask me, "What were you thinking about right before impact? Did your life flash before you? Did you think about your loved ones? Were you thinking about all the things you would miss?" No, no, and no. The only thing that I thought of was, "Shit, this is going to hurt!" At the moment of impact, I remember my car being thrown to the left side of the interstate as my car slid along the edge of a hill taking out pole after pole and the chains that were there to protect vehicles from going down into a ravine. What seemed like a nightmare that was never going to end lasted approximately fifteen seconds in total.

I remember being in a fog-like state. I looked around to see what had happened to the other vehicle. I was worried about the occupants of the other car and wanted to make sure they were okay. It was hard to see because every window of my car had been shattered. Suddenly, I saw the car that had hit me. It was in the middle of the road. Suddenly, I saw it back up and take off going the wrong way on the interstate. I reached down to grab my phone from the cup holder where I had last had it, but it was no longer there. I was a little frantic as I searched for it because I knew I had to call 911 to tell them that I had been hit by a car going the wrong way on the interstate and that it had continued to go the opposite way.

The next thing I knew, people were gathered around my car yelling at me to see if I was okay. I could see the traffic across the other interstate lanes opposite me had come to a complete stop to look at the wreckage. I soon realized they were looking at me. I could hear sirens off in the distance and eventually, police and firemen came to my assistance to pull me out of the car.

As I came around and became more aware of what had happened, I knew I had to call my family. Two of my kids were expecting me for dinner and I knew they would wonder why I had not shown up, especially since I had just spoken to them thirty minutes before, telling them I was on my way to meet them. I worried about how my youngest daughter would feel since she had called me earlier while I was on my way to tell me that she couldn't get in touch with her mother and she didn't have a way home from work. This resulted in my turning around and heading back to pick her up, only for her to call me ten minutes later to tell me that her mom was there but had not seen her. These events changed my timeline, putting me at the wrong place at the wrong time.

When bad things happen, we can question every moment, knowing that our lives are impacted, sometimes for the better and sometimes for the worse, based on decisions and events that change the time and/or location of our whereabouts. Life can remind us of our mortality on any given day and at any given moment. No one is promised tomorrow.

It's been six years since I was hit by a drunk driver who was a third-time offender. In the days following the accident, I can tell you I was scared to drive. I was anxious, nervous, overly worried, and hesitated to get behind the wheel of a car. I know the force of that impact has left me somewhat traumatized, which is why I still respond the way I do sometimes while I am driving. I do wonder if those triggers will ever subside.

In this chapter, I plan to focus on a different type of trauma. Not the type of trauma some educators have experienced or the type many of our students and families have had to live through. I would never want to minimize the horrific experiences some people have endured in their lifetime. This one is more systemic, and it is negatively impacting school cultures across the country daily. I will share the impact it is having and how it is causing people at all levels, in the classroom, building, and district office to hesitate. In addition, I will share how we can begin to heal by making some small shifts in our thinking, and more importantly, in our practices across all three levels.

Systemic Trauma

Systemic Trauma involves a complex series of events and interactions leading to both personal and professional psychological injuries to individuals, teams, and organizations. People will often blame themselves or point fingers at others as they cope with the anxiety, hurt, and/or pain that stems from their trauma. An outcome often overlooked is that individuals may even attempt to avoid the healing process and fall into cycles of poor or dysfunctional behavior. People generally are not trying to cause systemic trauma, but unfortunately, they may be stuck simply replicating poor past practices or acting in "survival mode" and cycling more trauma to others in the system.

Over the last five years. I have spent countless hours conducting cultural assessments for buildings: interviewing, observing, and working alongside students, teachers, parents, counselors, paraprofessionals, instructional coaches, librarians, custodians, kitchen staff, bus drivers, nurses, and, of course, building and district administrators to better understand their experiences both through my own lens as well as theirs.

With rare exceptions, teachers, support staff, and administrators begin by talking about how much they love the students. They share how much joy it brings them to watch their students grow academically and socially. They beam with pride when they talk about a student who early on showed no interest in school and now, months or years later, they get to cheer them across the stage as they receive their diploma.

Then suddenly it shifts. They begin to choose their words carefully, sometimes hesitating before they speak. A different tone slowly evolves in their voice as they begin to share their frustrations. They know what it takes to cultivate a culture of excellence in which students and staff alike look forward to coming to school–they can see it and they long for it. They want to have a voice; they want to feel valued and appreciated. Students, teachers, and administrators need clarity and better communication, and they want to know what is expected of them. They want to be great at what they do so they can make a positive difference in the lives of the students they serve and within the entire school community.

What Does It Look Like?

"What do you think the principal could have done differently in this situation?," I asked Sue.

"I don't know," she said. "This is the fourth principal West High has had in the last six years. Honestly, I don't think he is going to be able to change the culture around here."

"Why do you think that?" I asked Sue, who had served as the principal's administrative assistant for the last fifteen years.

She responded, "The teachers are tired and they are scared. No one knows what to do. They don't communicate at all. We are all walking on eggshells waiting for the other shoe to drop. We have all just kind of given up. I am not sure it is ever going to get better."

"Do you know what the principal expects of you?" I asked.

"If I am being honest, no. He doesn't tell me a whole lot," she replied.

Three hours and twelve staff interviews later, what I heard was similar to the experiences that had been shared with me countless times in many of the buildings I was serving at all levels. Students, teachers, support staff, and superintendents shared similar experiences of poor results and staff leaving. Many who wanted to help felt hopeless, wondering if one person could really make things better. That feeling led to widespread apathy, with people no longer believing that anything was going to change. Sue, as well as others, confided in me they were worried they were going to get in trouble if they made a mistake. "I just don't know what to do," said Sue. "I am scared to make a decision."

What Sue described was similar to the feedback we received from others. Students shared stories of teachers missing school. One young lady, in particular, complained about having had nine different substitute teachers in one month. She was concerned she was not going to be able to get the help she needed to prepare for the end-of-the-course final exam. She worried about her grade in the class and the effect it would have on her overall G.P.A. One principal expressed her frustration that the district office had announced via email they would be moving forward with a new math curriculum that had been planned. Although the district delayed the rollout by a semester, the principal was worried about the negative impact on her teachers and students.

Moreover, she felt the decision regarding the new curriculum had been driven by a board member and that neither she, nor her teachers, had been allowed to review or provide feedback on the changes.

Impact on People

Sue seemed confused when she entered the office and sat down to talk to me. She was also guarded. She stated she didn't know why I was there or why she had been selected. She also shared that she was not given any information about what the interview would entail. On the one hand, I found it interesting to hear this, especially since I felt we had communicated weeks in advance and sent the documents with detailed information that outlined the purpose for my visit and the steps that would be taken after the interviews were completed. We had also reached out by phone one week before the date to ensure everything was ready to go as planned. On the other hand, it was good for me to experience the breakdown in our communication so I could better understand its impact on people. I know during my tenure as principal there were plenty of times when I failed to communicate clearly, so by no means did I judge or have a right to judge. However, I also recognize the stress it places on others when we fail to communicate effectively or when we are not clear about our expectations.

I wanted people to be clear about the purpose of my visit, so I made sure to review the reason for my visit with each person. One shared with me that she had no idea who I was, but that she had heard from others I was a consultant who was there to help because the school was out of control. Another person shared that she felt the staff had lost confidence in the principal and they were hoping that another change might be taking place. That one hit me hard. I wondered what type of support the principal had been given. He had shared with me privately in an earlier conversation that there were a few staff members who had voiced their support for an internal candidate and were not happy when she was not given the job. And although it was evident that these feelings were prevalent among some staff in the building, according to this building principal it was neither acknowledged nor addressed before he came on board. Instead, as I described earlier in the book, he was given the keys and expected to lead without much direction or support.

These are real stories of real people who are negatively impacted daily in our schools. At times they are confused about what to do, which leads to high levels of stress because they don't feel they have any control over anything. Even veteran administrators and teachers can begin to question their ability to get the job done which can affect their confidence. When this impact is felt at all levels, whether a teacher in the classroom, a principal in the building, or a superintendent at the district office, it can have a negative ripple across the entire system, leaving the entire system feeling traumatized.

Below is an excerpt from a second-year junior high school principal who shared the following story with me regarding his experience as he transitioned into a new school. His story is similar to many others that have been shared with me regarding principals who are struggling to change the past practices that have existed in their schools, sometimes for years.

My first year as a 7-8 junior high principal was the year we all came back from Covid-19. During the year, I faced many challenges, including student mental health issues and students making poor choices related to social media. Students struggled with how to act after returning from distance learning. Many had been influenced by behaviors they had witnessed on television and on social media. We observed behaviors we had never seen before.

Consequently, I believed I needed to take swift action to address some of these issues to minimize the potential harm to students. Soon after, I received backlash that I did not anticipate. I felt hurt and couldn't understand why others were upset with me. I did my best to address the various situations I found myself in, with little support from my colleagues, including my assistant principals and supervisors.

In my conversations with them, I learned that they had become accustomed to working in isolation. Before my arrival, they had not been provided clear expectations for how to work as a team. Rather than follow clear and consistent processes and protocols, they had free rein to take care of their responsibilities on their own. As I worked to bring more systemic practices into place, I could sense their uneasiness. They admitted it was hard for them because the previous administration had encouraged and empowered them to make their own decisions. Now I was expecting them to check in with me and update me on their decisions. The more I pushed them, the more they seemed to resist. Looking back, I realize I expected them to make this shift too quickly. I felt it was my responsibility to protect them. I was worried that if we didn't follow specific processes it could potentially place us all in a precarious situation and I felt it was my responsibility to keep us out of any issues where we might be held liable.

As the year went on, I witnessed more and more behaviors where I perceived my colleagues were supporting kids to a fault. I was concerned that some of the actions that were being taken by my team were putting our students at risk. I became increasingly worried and I decided to go to my Director of Human Resources for support. This led to one of my administrators being placed on leave and eventually, the district parted ways with him. That decision was hard on all of us.

Months later, I am still paying for it. Although I believe I did the right thing, I still carry the label of being the person who got someone fired. Moreover, I continue to deal with equity issues due to the lack of processes and systems that have never been put in place. Most recently, this came to light again.

There was a racial incident that transpired in my school that impacted the entire school community. With the help of the district communications department, we were able to provide communication clearly and effectively. We worked with the high school to provide mentors to work with our students. We held parent nights and did our best to form community partnerships and even held listening meetings with students so they would feel loved and supported and that their voice was being heard. We worked tirelessly to denounce racism and educate all members of our school community. Overall, I felt that we did a good job handling a very difficult situation.

However, once again, I found myself in a position I wasn't sure how to handle. Other families in the district had heard how we had managed these incidents and began to inquire about open-enrolling their students in our school. This caused animosity among my fellow administrators. It started to seem like a competition between schools and not a collaboration. I struggled with this and started asking questions at the district level about the systems we had in place for such things. It was clear we were lacking a focus in this area, so I was asked to join several committees to support this work. Initially, there was a lot of excitement at the district level about creating and putting these practices into place.

After attending several meetings and reporting back to my fellow administrators, I learned that there was a lot of historical trauma that had happened before my arrival. These incidents caused my fellow administrators to distrust the district office staff which then led to a breakdown in systems and led buildings to operate in silos. I know we are on the right track and am hopeful that we will continue to work collectively as a community to put systems into place at all levels so that we can become a healthy district where teachers, principals, and district office leaders are aligned in their work.

This scenario is common when people within the system are not given clear expectations from which to teach and lead. The result is these individuals often find themselves trying to navigate their circumstances alone. When someone comes along and tries to instill a "new way of doing business," it can manifest itself as resentment towards those trying to bring about change. The response can come across as defensive, giving those trying to instill new processes the perception that they are not team players. These experiences have left some educators with a level of mistrust which causes them to retreat into isolated practices for fear of how others will view them. Over time, these isolated practices can lead to inequities in services provided to students and families across the districts.

This example could cause people to worry about the state of our schools. However, the good news is that most of what people describe during our cultural assessment interviews is positive. The words "family" and "community" are used often to describe a campus. Students talk positively about their friends, teachers, and coaches and, for the most part, share how much they like school, activities, and attending events. The majority of students describe feeling safe and having pride in their school. Teachers share how they love their students, appreciate their team members, and are grateful for the support they receive from their administration. Overall, the majority of teachers like what they do. Principals articulate how appreciative they are that their boss doesn't micromanage them and often brag that they have a great staff and how they love what they do, despite the challenges they face. And yet, it is still common to feel an undercurrent lurking below the surface that we cannot ignore if we want to create a healthy culture for every member of the school community.

Healthy System vs. Dysfunctional System

In the opening chapter, I stated that teachers, principals, and district office administration can all impact the climate and culture of an entire school community. In high-performing cultures, all three levels of the community are strategic and aligned in their practices. These three levels, or smaller communities: classroom, building, and district office—see themselves as one larger community. This larger community behaves as one and they are intentional in replicating processes, protocols, and frameworks at each level and across each community. We've seen these laid out in previous chapters (e.g., Power of Why x 3, Delegation, 1-2-4 Process, Perimeter Leadership vs. Inner Leadership, Managing Complex Conversations, & others). In each community, three areas affect the morale and performance of each staff member, which I have identified as *System - People - Fire.*

In a healthy system, each community is working on their system and working on their people the majority of the time, or more than 50%. High-performing cultures recognize that success lies in growing and developing their people. They invest time in them and work on their skillsets, mindsets, toolsets, and heart sets. By following this process, they minimize the number of daily fires, which can be exhausting. When they work on their people, they are simultaneously working on their system. With each undercurrent they mitigate or avoid altogether, they reduce their workload and, often, their stress level.

On the contrary, in an unhealthy system, each community works in isolation. They are independent of each other, fail to align their practices, rarely work on their system, and spend their time on the perimeter pointing fingers. Rather than work on their people, they blame them when they don't get the results they want. They find themselves so overwhelmed from putting out a multitude of fires that they rarely have time to grow and develop their people, thereby ignoring their larger systemic responsibilities. The lack of support many of these educators experience often leads to morale and performance issues. The illustration below depicts a healthy system and a dysfunctional system.

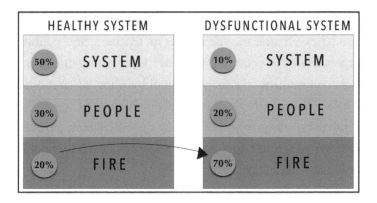

Notice in the second visual the percentage of time spent on fires. They are upside down compared to the healthy system. When administrators find themselves putting out a high number of fires, they are not able to find the necessary time to focus on their systems. After some time, this imbalance can become exhausting and weigh heavily on even the most positive leaders, eventually burning them out. I believe this is where many schools and campus leaders have landed and what is causing many to contemplate leaving the profession.

So what does it mean to work on the system and how do we work on our people so we can extinguish the fires to bring about a healthier system—a system in which we can thrive as a community together rather than wither away on our own? When we are aligned in our work, we can recalibrate our purpose so we can move beyond just sharing a plan, and, in addition, share results that inspire a community of learners.

A Systemic Recalibration

Imagine three columns side by side, each column representing a different community, and all three communities making up the entire system. For now, I want you to see this system as your current district. Within your district, you will find three levels or communities: classroom, school building, and district office. To function as a healthy system, these three communities will need to be aligned in their practices, model excellence, see themselves as teachers, and communicate clear expectations. For clarity purposes, I want you to understand that any single community, (classroom, school building, district office) also functions independently as an internal system and in some cases, two communities can come together to make up a smaller system, all within the larger system—that larger system being your entire school district. See the illustration below:

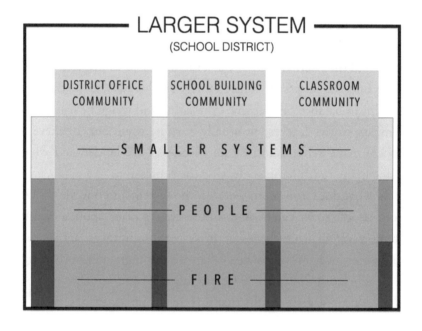

When we begin to examine these three areas in conjunction with one another, we can see the correlations and how one impacts the other. I believe that when we study the culture of any organization, we must begin at the top. Expecting Excellence (Core Principle 2) emphasizes modeling and remembering that we should never ask others to do what we are not willing to do ourselves. How can the district office ever ask the building or classroom community to model practices that they are not modeling themselves? Recalibration begins when the district office models effective behaviors, processes, and frameworks to cultivate a healthy system by expecting alignment and replication of the work across all communities.

Let's examine the three communities in depth so I can illustrate what it looks like when they are aligned and replicate one another. I have identified three specific areas at each level where you could begin to recalibrate your work so that you can get back to working on the system, working on your people, and preventing the fires. I have broken down these areas for each community in the image below:

LARGER SYSTEM
(SCHOOL DISTRICT)

DISTRICT OFFICE COMMUNITY	SCHOOL BUILDING COMMUNITY	CLASSROOM COMMUNITY
Strategic Plan	School Improvement Plan	Essential Learnings
Cabinet Team	Building Leadership Team	Collaborative Groups
Principal Voice	Staff Voice	Student Voice

P E O P L E

F I R E

District Office Community

It should be no surprise that I am beginning with this community. In my opinion, it always begins with leadership. Although I have never been a district office administrator, I worked for eleven different superintendents over a twenty-two-year span as a school leader and learned a tremendous amount under their mentoring. I recognize this is not the same as having district office experience, but I believe strongly that leadership is still about inspiring, influencing, and teaching others how to become better versions of themselves as teachers and leaders. Since leaving the full-time K-12 administration, I have been blessed to work side-by-side with many superintendents and district office staff and experience the complexities of their work through them. I am eternally grateful for those who embrace my support, seek advice, share their expertise with me, and allow me to observe them—sometimes in their most vulnerable state—so I can continue to learn and support them in addressing a variety of complex issues. I am truly humbled by their generosity. What I have learned from these experiences is that effective leaders are transparent leaders. They value the voice of others and seek their input regularly. They see themselves as teachers and are deliberate in building the capacity of others. Moreover, they are reflective, ask questions, and seek to learn from others.

The superintendents I have worked with have modeled these aforementioned attributes. With their support, I began to break down the critical work they were doing at the district level to understand their unique challenges. Together, we were able to identify three specific areas that make up their system so we could begin the process of reframing their work to get a better result when it came to the overall culture of the district, specifically as it pertained to staff morale:

DISTRICT-LEVEL SYSTEM:

<u>Strategic Plan</u> - Many school districts are invested in strategic planning, but the most successful districts are intentional in strategic doing. In some districts that were struggling, I observed lots of *idea sharing* but not a lot of *idea doing*. What I admired most about the superintendents I was working with was their willingness to share their experiences with me, including their successes and their failures. Of course, I also collected feedback through our assessments and interview process. Almost without exception, superintendents shared that the strategic plan was the area they felt they needed to focus on the most, as in this example:

In one particular district, Dr. Bernard shared how she spent an entire year seeking input from all stakeholders—school board, community members (businesses, support agencies, and families), cabinet members, principals, teachers, and support personnel. The most impressive part was that she also worked with principals to ensure that they repeated the same processes at the building levels to ensure that the staff voice didn't just come from a few representatives, but every staff member had a voice in terms of what they felt the district needed to include in the plan. Next, they followed the vision planning with action planning and once again reached out to seek input in terms of how to go about turning the vision ideas into actionable items, first at the macro, community level and then again at the micro, building level.

One regret she shared with me was that she had not sought input from students, and this bothered her. I share this vital piece for all of us to remember that people do the best they can and even when we try

> Many school districts are invested in strategic planning, but the most successful districts are intentional in strategic doing.

our best to do all things right, at times we will miss the mark. There are no perfect processes or actions to ensure a perfect result where everyone is satisfied. However, there are more effective ways to do things to get a better result. By all accounts in my findings when discussing the strategic plan process with staff members, they were very content with it. They appreciated the intentional efforts to give everyone a voice, the timeline (not rushed), the ongoing communication, and, most importantly, that they were focused on the work and moving forward with action, not just words. Dr. Bernard's process produced better results and minimized the undercurrents and in doing so, improved staff morale and improved the overall culture of the district.

Board and Cabinet Teams - Working with the school board was also a high priority for superintendents, especially since the Board serves as their boss, so probably a good thing that ranked high! The results were mixed when it came to them collaborating directly with their board members and cabinet team. Some were more intentional and made it a priority to work together, while in other districts, people were allowed to lead more independently. Interesting to note, I found a direct correlation between those who formally collaborated with their cabinet teams (regardless of the size of the district and size of the team) and those who did not when it came to communication. District personnel listed lack of communication as an issue more often when superintendents failed to meet regularly with their cabinet members.

Principal Voice - The one area I was surprised that was not mentioned more often was the importance of growing and developing their building leaders. Those who did mention this as a priority, saw themselves as a support system for principals to do their job, but not necessarily in developing their leadership skills. Most mentioned that they sought input when they felt it was necessary, but not in a formal way. Even Dr. Bernard shared that although she knew the importance of growing her building principals, she had not been deliberate enough in doing so, but assured me she was going to invest more time focusing on that moving forward.

School Building Community

I will admit that I have a soft spot for the building leader. I am not going to apologize for that. You don't spend twenty-two years serving in that role without walking away with a significant amount of battle scars that would make even the strongest of MMA fighters question their toughness. I am very familiar with the daily obstacles that my colleagues face in their work, navigating the many duties that come with the position that some days can seem insurmountable. My intent is not to minimize the significant challenges my fellow leaders face regardless of their job responsibility in the school district. A lifetime is not enough to master all the challenges we face. It is simply that I can empathize easier with the emotional toll they experience having been through it myself for over two decades.

However, the compassion I feel for my fellow principals does not prevent me from maintaining the highest standards for their work. Truthfully, I am inclined to expect more from them because I know the impact they can have on others, including students, families, and their colleagues. I am grateful they allow me to serve them in that capacity.

First, I encourage building administrators to see themselves as one part of a system within the larger system. With that comes three very important responsibilities, the first being to *Carry the Banner* for their district office colleagues at all times. When building leaders speak negatively about the district office staff, it hurts the relationship with their administrative colleagues and promotes mistrust. If all three communities are modeling this behavior, it can quickly fragment the system. Second, they must be intentional in aligning their systemic practices with those of the district office with integrity. Part of the systemic practices will require them to commit to working on their people whenever they find themselves in the fire. Third, to accept that there will be times when their district office colleagues lose their focus and disregard their systemic responsibilities. When this happens (because we can predict it will), building leaders must stay the course and continue to work on their internal systems within the larger system. Effective building leaders are not critical of another community within the system. Instead, they focus on controlling what they can control and that is to ensure they continue to model a system of excellence within their community:

BUILDING-LEVEL SYSTEM:

School Improvement Plan - Like their superintendent counterparts, building leaders must establish clear and measurable building goals. This is best accomplished when a process includes input from all stakeholders. High-performing schools empower their building leadership teams to work with their colleagues to review the strategic plan. Together, they identify targeted areas that align with the plan to address the average that exists in their school community and include these areas as part of their overall school improvement plan. Every staff member clearly understands the reasons for needing to address specific issues, is invested, and can articulate to others the reasons for the changes in a positive way:

> Curtis was in his fourth year as an elementary school principal when he contacted me in late October. He told me his superintendent had emailed him to tell him that a few staff members had reached out to him to express their concerns about his school improvement plan and that he had asked to meet with him the next day. During our conversation, Curtis admitted that he was struggling to take his vision and get "buy-in" from his staff. After three years, he felt he was ready to take his team

and school to the next level. As we broke down the process, it was clear that Curtis had bypassed some important steps.

Curtis described how he had shared his vision with the faculty at the back-to-school kickoff. He had worked on his presentation throughout the summer and had asked his assistant principal for input on any issues he felt needed to be addressed. He believed the staff meeting had gone well and that they seemed engaged, but it had not generated much discussion. Not wanting to control the entire meeting, he reminded everyone to see him if they had any questions and that he would be sharing more information as the year progressed. When I asked about the feedback he had received, he admitted that only a few teachers had commented and they were supportive of his ideas. This led him to further believe that his entire staff was supportive. When I inquired about the steps he had taken since the kickoff to work on his vision, he indicated he had been swamped with the beginning-of-the-year tasks and had not made a lot of progress. He did share that he had spent time discussing his plan in more detail with his leadership team and that they were working on a few of the items, but he hadn't had a chance to find out how things were progressing. By the end of the call, I could tell that Curtis was questioning himself and was worried about his meeting with the superintendent. I did my best to help him reframe the situation and see it as his superintendent wanting to support him rather than punish him.

The experience described thus far is quite common. I would even say that I could identify with it because I lived it. Principals who are ready to take their schools to the next level use the summer months when they finally catch their breath to script out a draft, get excited thinking this is what everyone wants, and kick off a year by announcing a new plan. Once school begins it can quickly become a "We will get to it when we can" plan because of all the fires that are burning. As I reflect on Curtis's story, I cannot help but wonder how his experience would have been different had he worked for Dr. Bernard. I worry that too many principals are still being handed the keys and expected to successfully carry out a vision on their own without much guidance.

By the end of last year, Curtis was still addressing the undercurrents he created, but he learned a lot, mainly about the importance of giving his staff a voice in the process and building the plan *with* them rather than building it *for* them. The good news is he had fostered enough credibility and support because of his genuine heart, his work ethic, his support for his teachers, and his love for kids. This served him well and he was allowed to recover from his missteps, and together Curtis and I were able to recalibrate and make the necessary adjustments to get him back on track. As we approach a new school year, Curtis now has a detailed plan describing how, together with his staff, they will move forward and produce better results.

Building Leadership Team - As we learned back in Chapter 3, empowering a community of leaders to help you lead can be a game-changer for any building leader. Effective principals utilize their building teams as a support system to work towards implementing building goals. When Curtis bypassed this step, he quickly found himself in recovery mode, trying to put out fires. Had he sought support from his leadership team, they would have helped him identify potential undercurrents. Instead, he worked on the plan independently, seeking only minimal input from his assistant principal during the summer. Scheduling bi-weekly building leadership team meetings help to build leadership capacity, elicit input regularly, and improve communication across the school community.

Staff Voice - Meeting with the building leadership team more frequently allows for more opportunities to collect feedback from various school leaders. It also opens the door for other potential issues that could cause problems for morale and the overall culture. This stems from building leaders leaning too much on the same people. This can create an under-current of favoritism and resentment if other staff feel that only a few voices are being heard. This will require transparency, communication, and an intentional effort by building principals to model the way if they expect teacher leaders to replicate the same process in collecting feedback from colleagues to make them feel that their voice is just as important to the decision-making process. Staff meetings can also be revamped by assigning building leadership members to specific teams to gather feed-back in small group settings to give all staff a collective voice.

Classroom Community

Last fall I was doing classroom observations with the principal when I met a teacher who left an impression on me. He described Susan as a master third-grade teacher who was respected by her peers. For over twenty years, she worked hard to master her craft. She built strong relationships with students, created meaningful and engaging lessons, and did her best to help each child feel confident and capable so they could experience success. It was important to Susan that all her stu-dents learn the material and demonstrate their mastery of learning on assessments. Although some of her students were grouped, rotating periodically so they could connect, she had mastered a system whereby she allowed students to work independently, while those who needed additional support had access to her for support

Her colleague Beth, down the hall, was struggling in her tenth year as a teacher. This was her third building and her first year teaching third grade. The principal shared that he had received approximately a dozen requests from parents to have Susan as their child's teacher. During our conversation, the principal shared that he had moved Beth from first to third grade, hoping that Susan's influence would be good for her. He told me that he often had to "stay on her" to teach the standards the building was working on and that she struggled to identify the needs of her students to understand why they were not grasping the material. Moreover, her classroom management skills were lacking which resulted in additional issues with behavior and high numbers of student referrals.

CLASSROOM SYSTEM:

Essential Learnings - Healthy systems consist of all three communities using the majority of their time to work on their system. Similar to their building and district-level counterparts, classroom communities align their work by focusing on their essential learnings. Essential learnings are those learnings that are tied to core standards. These learnings are often focused on outcomes, with teachers working toward higher levels of understanding which helps identify which students need additional supports put into place. It was clear that Susan and Beth were not aligned in identifying the essential learnings for all third graders, nor were they aligned in their instructional or relationship-building strategies. To be fair, both would have needed support from the building principal to ensure this happened.

Collaborative Groups - When implemented effectively, group work brings many benefits to the classroom environment, including increased social connections, on-task behaviors, greater confidence, increased peer support, and improved learning to name just a few. It was evident that Susan had mastered the art of having students work independently and collaboratively. She shared that over the years she learned from her students that at times they preferred to work alone and other times with peers, which led to students the day I visited, having a choice of doing one of the other or going back and forth throughout the period.

As for Beth, the classroom was set up in traditional rows. Students were reminded on more than one occasion not to talk unless they raised their hands and were called on. While it was hard for me to initially locate Susan when I walked into her classroom, Beth sat at the front of the room and worked from a digital camera to project problems on the whiteboard for the majority of the time I visited. It is important to note that instruction some may deem "traditional" is not an indicator that learning is not taking place. However, we must also acknowledge that for many students, this structure, when used consistently over a long period, will eventually lead to other behavioral and learning issues for students.

Student Voice - We have seen in the other two systems that when voice is not factored into the equation, a negative undercurrent is often manifested. Student voice is no exception. Classroom communities that emphasize students' voices, create fewer undercurrents and, therefore, healthier classroom cultures. As Susan shared, she learned over the years by listening to students' feedback that she was able to create an environment in which students had a choice to work either independently or collaboratively. Whether we are talking about student choice or determining classroom agreements, my experience has been this: in classrooms where students are given a voice in what something will look like, it frequently results in a better outcome when it comes to how students view their experience in the classroom and whether they carry the banner for the teacher in a positive way.

When we look at the three communities above we can see how they are focused on their systems within their communities, and the correlations between the three. When we are deliberate in our attempt to align and replicate these systems—in this case, strategic plan, school improvement plan, and essential learnings—we begin to recalibrate our work together across the entire system.

We learned earlier that if we want to cultivate a healthy system, we must spend more than 50% of the time working on our systems within each community. If you recall, that percentage also includes time spent working on our people. Let's take a more extensive look at what it means to work on your people.

LARGER SYSTEM
(SCHOOL DISTRICT)

DISTRICT OFFICE COMMUNITY	SCHOOL BUILDING COMMUNITY	CLASSROOM COMMUNITY
Strategic Plan	School Improvement Plan	Essential Learnings
Cabinet Team	Building Leadership Team	Collaborative Groups
Principal Voice	Staff Voice	Student Voice
Connections	Relationships	Capacity
Engagement	Processess	Frameworks
Confidence	Skillsets	Mindsets

FIRE

PEOPLE:

Effective teachers and leaders never forget they are teachers first. They are intentional when it comes to teaching. They invest time in their people. They are connectors and work hard to earn the trust of their people so they can better understand and utilize their talents to build capacity. Teachers and leaders who are more intentional in teaching and coaching their people rather than just directing or expecting them to figure it out find that they get better overall production from their students and team and, therefore, better results in terms of productivity and overall morale. When students and staff are not meeting expectations, reframe it and see it differently. Rarely is anyone trying to let others down intentionally. If the task or job that we have asked them to do did not get done or did not meet our expectations in terms of quality, spend more time working on your people and teach them how to do it better.

There will always be fires to put out. By reframing situations, you will begin to see the fires not as moments of despair, but as opportunities. A "firetunity" of sorts, for growth, both for the person who created the fire and for the person trying to put the flames out. Let's be intentional in learning more about the cause of the fires we encounter in education.

LARGER SYSTEM
(SCHOOL DISTRICT)

DISTRICT OFFICE COMMUNITY	SCHOOL BUILDING COMMUNITY	CLASSROOM COMMUNITY
Strategic Plan	School Improvement Plan	Essential Learnings
Cabinet Team	Building Leadership Team	Collaborative Groups
Principal Voice	Staff Voice	Student Voice
Connections	Relationships	Capacity
Engagement	Processess	Frameworks
Confidence	Skillsets	Mindsets
Lack of Engagement	Conflict Management	School Issues
Classroom Disruptions	Student Discipline	Parent Complaints
Student Apathy	Managerial Tasks	Personnel Issues

FIRE:

Teachers and leaders who spend their time putting out fires all day will tell you it is frustrating and leaves them feeling physically spent and often defeated. The more time spent in the fire, the less time there is to work on the system and your people. Fires are ignited every day. That is the nature of our work because we are dealing with unpredictable variables. As exhausting as these fires can be, they can also be rewarding. People who start fires for the most part do so unintentionally. They are not arsonists. In most cases, they do not see how their actions lead to the fires you often find yourself trying to extinguish. Reframe it and see it differently. The fire is telling you who among your staff you need to work on and as you do so, they will tell you what part of the system needs your attention and leadership. Then teach your people how to operate within the intended system designed. Use the fires as an opportunity to teach; jump into the fire and rather than focus on putting out the flames, focus instead on helping them understand how they started the fire and teach them the processes and frameworks that I have shared throughout this book to support them in their growth so they learn to avoid igniting the fires.

The following is an excerpt from a current superintendent who has been intentional and transparent in moving towards a systemic structure throughout the district that is rooted in processes, protocols, and frameworks where people are given a voice, empowered to lead, and treated with compassion and empathy to bring their best to work every day:

> I currently serve as superintendent of a school district with an enrollment of over 13,000 students. Three years ago, we set out to implement a comprehensive systems approach that would assist us in defining our roles as responsibilities and decision-making processes, and help us identify our collective strengths and weaknesses as an administrative leadership team.

Much has changed in the three years since we began this important work, including our roles within the system and our systems approach to our strategic plan. Our work has been filled with complex conversations, tears, frustrations, and celebrations. My hope is that our data will reflect positive results based on our collective commitments to each other. A part of this commitment has entailed us providing honest feedback about what we are doing well and what needs improvement.

My critical work has revolved around the development and publication of a comprehensive strategic plan. Strategic alignment of goals, strategy, and metrics are systems processes that are more complex. Our Mission, Vision, Values, and Portrait of a Learner required strategic and complex investments in our staff and our strategic partners. The investment in internal and/or external human capital was essential in giving everyone a voice to help us lead this charge.

By giving everyone a voice, the leadership team embraced the following conceptual understandings:

1. We all lead from our strengths.
2. We all will fail.
3. When we do fail, the team will be present to pick us up and carry our banner.

We also unfailingly embraced:

1. Who we are - Our Mission, Vision, and Values
2. Why we do what we do - Our Portrait of a Learner
3. The Way and How we do it - Our Excellences
4. How we are accountable - Our Governance and Accountability Model.

One might assume, as I did, that we should start by empowering our people. Although empowerment is fundamental and appears obvious, I missed the initial investment in strong processes that drive structure and transparency. Our strategic External Partner (EP) conducted an audit and advised that it was best to start by teaching the cabinet—Assistant Superintendents, Business and Operations Manager, Human Relations Director, and me—the importance of effective processes. Essential in this audit was the unwavering commitment to valuing all leaders and building relationships focused on growth, both personally and professionally.

Our EP worked diligently with our frontline leaders, teaching them and us the power of effective processes. They worked hard to connect the process back to our values as an organization. Outcomes related to a refined/recalibrated process included a clear understanding of expectations and transparency in operations from the district office into buildings and vice versa. When building-level principals embraced the work of utilizing these processes, their comments included "it really made a difference in engagement and productivity during our staff meetings." The relational aspect of the process was inherent in our EP's approach to teaching and learning which is founded in a culture of investment and excellence. It was also evident and predictable when some leaders initially resisted the idea of implementing the processes. Relationships take time and with time comes trust. Consistent modeling of processes and relationships that focused on our values opened the door to resistors.

We learned many lessons throughout our recalibration with our EP, which included highly specific feedback, open honest communication, listening and questioning protocols, and the influence of processes, frameworks, and transparency. This initial investment started and ended with compassion for everyone. It was highly personal yet professional at every level. A highly specific process was always the outcome but it yielded stronger relationships, finding the strengths of each individual and empowering all to lead through our collective values.

Routine, consistency, structure, and alignment are embedded in a healthy system. We have started to reap the reward of a strong strategic plan because we embraced our values, defined our processes, valued people for who they are, and empowered them to lead at each level within our school community. It started with an EP and his courage to question our process and offer suggestions to reframe a new path forward.

When teachers, principals, and/or superintendents are intentional in working on their systems, it elevates a belief across a campus that anything can be accomplished. It is critical that each community–classroom, school, and district–focus on the *why* and the *what* of the work to bring about a clear vision for what needs to happen, but it is the *how (processes, frameworks, and systems)* that makes the vision become a reality. Having had a front row seat to the district above, I was able to observe the following: the investment in relationships, the emphasis placed on valuing people, and a standard of excellence placed on expectations for everyone in the organization, that set the stage for an overdue recalibration.

Reference

Jobs, Steve. Stanford News. Commencement Speech, 2005)

Reflect AND
RECALIBRATE

(Use the following space for reflective notes)

CHAPTER 6

Conclusion

*A great teacher and leader changes everything. Ask any student or
staff member who has had one. They will tell you it matters.
You can be that person.*

The story goes that in 1912 Jim Thorpe, a Native American
from Oklahoma, was representing the U.S in track & field
at the Olympics. On the morning of his competition, his
shoes went missing. He ended up finding one shoe in a garbage can and
someone else gave him another. But one of the shoes was too big, so
he had to wear extra socks to make them fit. Wearing these shoes, Jim
Thorpe went on to win two gold medals.

Many educators are struggling right now, trying to understand all
that has happened in the past few years and wondering if it will ever be
the same as it was before the pandemic. It would be easy to think of a
hundred excuses why we are holding back, to place blame, to be scared,
or maybe even be angry. I don't begrudge anyone who is feeling this
way. It is okay to have such feelings and in some ways, it may give us a
release from it all. However, life throws us curve balls and this one just

happened to come with a vicious sinker as well. But I ask you, "Now what?" Whatever you are dealing with—stolen shoes, family drama, lost income, isolation, or you feel like your flame is slowly dying out—don't let it stop you from running your race. I know this: We will all have more difficult experiences and more daunting challenges, but we cannot allow these times to redefine how we want to live our best lives. We can choose to *behave our way to a better day.*

At the end of each school year, I see my educator friends pushing their minds and bodies to the very last day, squeezing out every last ounce of energy they have left in reserve. Once the students walk out those school doors and head home for the summer, they can finally lean back and exhale deeply, knowing full well they have experienced something special. They can breathe again. It takes a few warm summer days to recalibrate their hearts, their minds, and their passion for teaching and leading as they look back on the year and appreciate all they have accomplished. It's in those moments where they recapture their spirit because their minds have come to a slow pause and they can process all the good that has taken place and it reignites a renewed sense of purpose for the work again.

Before they know it, a new school year is right around the corner. If you have worked any amount of time in education, you know that the passion and energy that you kicked off the school year with will begin to subside around the beginning of October and again around late February as the challenges continue to mount throughout the year. If we can predict this, then maybe it is time to be more strategic and take time to come together as a staff and recalibrate. We do so in August and May, but we often forget the critical months during the school year. I am encouraging district leaders, building leaders, and classroom teachers to take time to recalibrate periodically during the year. Our students and staff need to come together to be intentional in identifying all that has been accomplished every few months so that it may bring a newfound sense of hope and positively impact morale. This will allow you to also reframe your thinking, to see things differently, and by doing so, influence you to change yourself to generate better results.

Culturize **Investment Plan**

I hope that the 4 Premises of *Culturize* will serve as a framework for you moving forward to recalibrate you in your work, regardless of your title or position, and to assist you in reframing your thinking so you can bring a better version of yourself to every conversation and every interaction:

1. Lead from a core set of values.

2. Cultivate a community of leaders.

3. See the culture through the eyes of others.

4. Average exists in every organization.

When I look back, I know that is what Jim did for me. I was fortunate that I was able to recalibrate once a month every time he returned to my building. The questions he asked, and the way he challenged me to see my students, families, and staff differently, helped me reframe my thinking. Although I may not currently serve in that same capacity for you, I hope this book has influenced your thinking and reframed your mindset, given you the confidence to believe that you can develop the proper skillsets, and provided you with the necessary tools to begin implementing more effective processes and frameworks immediately, and inspired you to see things through your heart as well as your eyes to better equip you and your colleagues as you continue this critical work.

Regardless of the time of year you currently find yourself in, I hope that you reflect on Jim and his questioning: "What if it's us?" and pay close attention to the way you are responding by using the *Power of Why x 3* Framework to remember that we can all lose our passion for the work at times. Be clear about the reasons for the change you want to see, and invest time in people to better understand their behavior so you can help them grow.

As we walk the building, let's make sure that our actions reflect the words on the signs hanging on our walls so they don't lose meaning. Let's ensure that all kids—yes, even ones like Max, who we met earlier—are being treated fairly and all adults in the school care about them. If kindness matters, then let's show others just how much it does.

Remember that staff morale is impacted each time we add things to their plate, but it suffers even more when we don't foster a relationship with them that shows them how much we care. Take care of your people.

Jim reminded me we are all susceptible to perimeter thinking and that we must pull back from the edges and back towards our inner selves. If we want to be better for the Pam's of the world, then we can't blame them when something goes wrong. A poor process will almost always equate to a poor result.

Building capacity requires an intentional commitment to our processes and frameworks to make certain we set our people up for success. Meeting protocols, delegation coaching cycles, a 1-2-4 framework, building consensus, and managing complex conversations are tools that you can use to help you maximize positive results.

To avoid the potential undercurrents, we must first recognize that we are often the primary undercurrent. It is often our words, reactions, behaviors, and practices that pull us below the surface. Anonymous surveys, committees, delegation, managing student behaviors, and other common practices all carry the potential for deep undercurrents when introduced ineffectively.

When we elevate our response to levels 8-10 for the majority of the incidents that occur in school, we influence others to do the same, leaving a trail of stressed-out employees stretched out across the campus. Let's commit to doing our best to pause, reflect, and see issues in our school from a healthier lens.

The transition period for students and staff is hard. Therefore, we must establish clear protocols and expectations as part of the onboarding process to support all students and colleagues as they enter our schools. It is unacceptable for Instructional Coaches like Sam to want to return to their previous position four months into a new position because she didn't feel supported.

If we fail to be intentional in aligning our work across the larger system and we ignore the important areas of working on our systems and working on our people, we will remain upside down as we continue to fight the fires. These fires will continue to consume our work and eventually burn us out, leaving our systems fragmented and traumatized. We cannot afford to continue to lose dream chasers like Xavier because of the average that exists in our organization.

And finally, the imperfections in our behavior and the imperfections in our lives should not be a source of discouragement for us. We can choose to be better versions of ourselves tomorrow and into next year. The choice remains up to us as to what impact we will leave on those we encounter at home and within our organization. Every day we should ask ourselves, "What will be our legacy?" Do we see ourselves as a source of happiness and joy for the organization and those around us?

Your occupation is what you do, not who you are. If you let it define you, you'll lose your way. I believe educators need to be intentional about getting back to the joy of the work—the joy of building our people and our systems. Choose to not merely break the cycle, but to also work toward *healing* your family tree. As you do so, you will have more conviction in your purpose to serve others in your life that you touch both personally and professionally. Few people can "self-care" their way out of trauma. So, we need "Community Care" for the individuals and organizations that have experienced systemic trauma. Are we connected and empathetic to the joys as well as the suffering of those we serve?

As teachers and leaders, we may not have caused the dysfunction that created systemic trauma, but it is our responsibility to lead the healing of the organization. Unless we look at the source of pain and suffering in our organization, as well as our shortcomings, we will be unable to find the desire and the vision of what we could become and must become for our students, staff, and the community we serve. For when you're in the fire and operating from a core set of values, you will have the perspective and energy to work on your people and systems.

Through this work, we will improve our processes, systems, and frameworks. Our people and organization need us to turn our gaze away from the dysfunction of the system and bring our energy and focus back on systemic recalibration.

Live a Great Story

One of my all-time favorite quotes by Ralph Waldo Emerson reads as follows:

> "Write it on your heart that every day is the best day in the year. He is rich who owns the day, and no one owns the day who allows it to be invaded with fret and anxiety. Finish every day and be done with it. You have done what you could. Some blunders and absurdities, no doubt crept in. Forget them as soon as you can, tomorrow is a new day; begin it well and serenely, with too high a spirit to be cumbered with your old nonsense. This new day is too dear, with its hopes and invitations, to waste a moment on the yesterdays."

We know how insanely crazy the educational landscape has been over the last few years. Leading our classrooms and leading our schools has been beyond hectic; it has beaten up some of the best in our profession and left many feeling that they can no longer do this work. To our former colleagues who have left the profession, let's thank them for giving it their all and taking their game to another venue to make their impact on our profession.

If you are still hanging in there, consider yourself a badass! You have control over where you decide to go from here. I hope that this book will inspire you to want to change your story. No one ever said that being an educator would be easy, but if we take time to look around and see all that we have rather than what we do not have, I believe it's certainly worth it. At the end of the day, regardless of the obstacles that come our way, it is our choice what story we want to live so let's live a great one.

In conclusion, I am here to tell you that you can capture lightning in the bottle again—that feeling you felt when you sat in the interview chair and you visualized yourself changing the trajectory of the life of a child. It's time to get out of this rut and recalibrate our why, our work, our values, ourselves, and each other. By working collectively, strategically, and systemically, we can begin to heal. I invite you to join me in *culturizing* that feeling again.

Want to rekindle your passion for working in schools? Then as Jim taught me, you will need to reframe your thinking and see your work…

+ Not as a *responsibility*, but as an *opportunity*.

+ Not as a *task*, but as a *mission*.

+ Not as an *obligation*, but as a *purpose*.

+ Not as a *burden*, but as a *blessing*

…and watch how your life starts changing today.

It is time. Time to *Recalibrate Our Culture*!

Reflect AND
RECALIBRATE

(Use the following space for reflective notes)

Acknowledgements

To Marianne, Aj, Miraya, and Marisa. Thank you for your unconditional love, for always believing in me, and for never giving up on me.

To Paul and Gloria Casas. Thank you, Mom and Dad, for instilling in me that through hard work and a belief in myself, anything is possible.

To Paul, Nikki, David, and Leslie. Thank you for your continued support and for always carrying my banner.

To Kheila, James, and Jack. Thank you for giving me a chance. For seeing the best in me. For loving me and inviting me into your family.

I love you all.

About the Author

Jimmy Casas has been an educator for over 30 years, serving twenty-two years as a school leader, including fourteen years as Principal at Bettendorf High School. Under his leadership, Bettendorf was named one of the Best High Schools in the country three times by Newsweek and US News & World Report.

Jimmy was named the 2012 Iowa Secondary Principal of the Year and was selected as runner-up NASSP 2013 National Secondary Principal of the Year. In 2014, Jimmy was invited to the White House to speak on the Future Ready Schools pledge. Jimmy is also the author of eight books, including the best-selling books *Culturize: Every Student. Every Day. Whatever It Takes, Live Your Excellence: Bring Your Best Self to School Every Day, and Handle with Care: Managing Difficult Situations in Schools with Dignity and Respect.*

Jimmy is the owner and CEO of J Casas & Associates, where he serves as a professional leadership coach for school leaders across the country. In January 2020, Jimmy launched ConnectEDD, a publishing company aimed at giving back to the profession by supporting educators to become published authors. Connect with Jimmy at JimmyCasas.com and on Twitter and Instagram: Casas_Jimmy

More from
ConnectEDD Publishing

Since 2015, ConnectEDD has worked to transform education by empowering educators to become better-equipped to teach, learn, and lead. What started as a small company designed to provide professional learning events for educators has grown to include a variety of services to help teachers and administrators address essential challenges. ConnectEDD offers instructional and leadership coaching, professional development workshops focusing on a variety of educational topics, a roster of nationally recognized educator associates who possess hands-on knowledge and experience, educational conferences custom-designed to meet the specific needs of schools, districts, and state/national organizations, and ongoing, personalized support, both virtually and onsite. In 2020, ConnectEDD expanded to include publishing services designed to provide busy educators with books and resources consisting of practical information on a wide variety of teaching, learning, and leadership topics. Please visit us online at connecteddpublishing.com or contact us at: info@connecteddpublishing.com

Recent Publications:

Live Your Excellence: Action Guide by Jimmy Casas

Culturize: Action Guide by Jimmy Casas

Daily Inspiration for Educators: Positive Thoughts for Every Day of the Year by Jimmy Casas

Eyes on Culture: Multiply Excellence in Your School by Emily Paschall

Pause. Breathe. Flourish. Living Your Best Life as an Educator by William D. Parker

L.E.A.R.N.E.R. Finding the True, Good, and Beautiful in Education by Marita Diffenbaugh

Educator Reflection Tips Volume II: Refining Our Practice by Jami Fowler-White

Handle With Care: Managing Difficult Situations in Schools with Dignity and Respect by Jimmy Casas and Joy Kelly

Disruptive Thinking: Preparing Learners for Their Future by Eric Sheninger

Permission to be Great: Increasing Engagement in Your School by Dan Butler

Daily Inspiration for Educators: Positive Thoughts for Every Day of the Year, Volume II by Jimmy Casas

The 6 Literacy Levers: Creating a Community of Readers by Brad Gustafson

The Educator's ATLAS: Your Roadmap to Engagement by Weston Kieschnick

In This Season: Words for the Heart by Todd Nesloney, LaNesha Tabb, Tanner Olson, and Alice Lee

Leading with a Humble Heart: A 40-Day Devotional for Leaders by Zac Bauermaster

ConnectEDD PUBLISHING

Made in United States
Troutdale, OR
06/23/2023

10736116R00096